Praise for *Healing Anxiety, Depression and Unw*

"This book presents cutting-edge interventions to relieve distress and suffering using simple mindfulness and yoga practices. It is written in a warm, compassionate voice that guides the reader and makes each step easy and sequential. There are many workbooks now available to both clients and therapists, but this is one of the best!"

- Janina Fisher, PhD
Assistant Education Director, Sensorimotor Psychotherapy Institute,
author of *Healing the Fragmented Selves of Trauma Survivors*

"A calm mind, emotional aliveness, self-compassion-these are the qualities of resilience that so many struggle to find. They are also the promises of this jewel of a book. Blending modern neuroscience with ancient healing practices, Mary NurrieStearns makes it crystal clear how to apply mindfulness and yoga skills for resilient mental health. Read it, practice it and create your own joyful life."

- Henry Emmons, MD
co-founder of NaturalMentalHealth.com and
author of *The Chemistry of Joy and The Chemistry of Calm*

"Mary has succinctly combined relevant literature from neuroscience, brain development, family and cultural studies, clinical work, and personal experience. The result is a valuable tool for a clinician or an individual wanting to know what to do, and also understand why. Her gentle coaching style is both supportive and inspiring. This is a very practical workbook of small, doable, and pleasant steps to take. When done persistently, they will change the brain and result in increased happiness, well-being and sense of self-worth in one's life. There is much hope in these actionable skills."

- Lindsay Patterson, PhD

"With joyful clarity and wisdom, Mary NurrieStearns has distilled 38 years of professional practice and personal experience into a concise and coherent guide for healing. I highly recommend this invaluable resource, and I will use it daily in my personal life and clinical practice."

- Cindy Reynolds, PhD

Healing Anxiety, Depression and Unworthiness

78 Brain-Changing Mindfulness & Yoga Practices

Mary NurrieStearns, MSW, LCSW, C-IAYT

Copyright © 2018 Mary NurrieStearns

Published by:

PESI Publishing & Media
PESI, Inc
3839 White Ave
Eau Claire, WI 54703

Cover: Amy Rubenzer
Editing: Blair Davis
Photography: Leslie Hoyt
Layout: Amy Rubenzer & Bookmasters

ISBN: 9781683731498

Proudly printed in the United States of America

PESI
Publishing
& Media
www.publishing.pesi.com

About the Author

Mary NurrieStearns, MSW, LCSW, C-IAYT

Mary NurrieStearns draws on more than 38 years as a mental health professional and 28 years of meditation and yoga practice. She is an advanced-level yoga teacher, certified yoga therapist, and ordained member of Thich Nhat Hahn's Order of Interbeing.

She is author of the *Daily Meditations for Healing and Happiness* card deck (2016), co-author of *Yoga Mind, Peaceful Mind* (2015), *Yoga for Emotional Trauma* (2013), and *Yoga for Anxiety* (2010), and co-editor of *Soulful Living*. Mary was the former editor of *Personal Transformation* magazine. She has produced audio CDs on the healing practices of self-compassion and meditation and DVDs on yoga for emotional trauma and anxiety.

She teaches yoga classes and seminars across the United States and co-leads, with her husband, transformational meditation and yoga retreats. Mary has suffered from anxiety and emotional trauma and credits mindfulness practices for profound personal transformation.

To contact Mary or for information, visit www.PersonalTransformation.com.

Contents

Acknowledgements

No one exists autonomously, and no book is written solely by its author. This workbook is truly the result of the efforts of many. I give thanks to the people mentioned below and to numerous unnamed others who helped this workbook come into being. I begin with Claire Zelasko, certifications manager at Evergreen Certifications, who encouraged me to make a workbook proposal to PESI Publishing after hearing how close this subject matter is to my heart. Karsyn Morse, my acquisitions editor, offered fine counsel that improved the workbook concept, and the publishing staff transformed the manuscript into a workbook.

I am indebted to remarkable patients and students who trusted me to teach them about the healing power of mindfulness approaches. A few of their stories are in the workbook. Of course, their names and facts about their lives are altered to protect their confidentiality. I could easily have told stories about other patients, as I have had the privilege of witnessing extraordinary human resiliency. Additionally, I bow to those patients with trauma histories who allowed me to work with them when I was younger and not yet trained in mindfulness. They taught me the limitations of therapeutic approaches not based on brain science and mindfulness of body and mind, which are newer in the field of mental health.

Advancements in psychotherapeutic interventions rely on research. Accordingly, I acknowledge the scientists who built the foundation for the evidenced-based approaches presented in this workbook. I give thanks to mindfulness experts who wrote about the application of mindfulness in clinical settings.

Much appreciation to Leslie Hoyt, the photographer who made the photo shoot a joy, and to the yoga model, Lindsay Schuler Garbelman, who is beautiful inside and outside. I bow in gratitude to my friend Bridget Blomfield for reading the first and second of three drafts of the manuscript. She loyally slogged through rough writing, continuously supplied me with love, and encouraged me to include clinical stories. I bow in gratitude to my friend Terry Vincent for reading the second draft, offering beneficial critical feedback, and encouraging me to connect with you by sharing about myself.

Finally, I thank my family. My nieces and nephew believed in me, and my siblings cheered me on. They all waited faithfully for me to be more available again. My wonderful husband rubbed my shoulders well over a hundred times as I sat at my computer keyboard pecking away. He gave me the space to write and also held me to my promises that we would visit family, take vacation, and have a life beyond my office, yoga studio, and writing. He kept food in the kitchen and contributed his love and knowledge to the workbook.

Introduction

No one wishes for the anxiety and depression that many of us personally know. Undoubtedly, my own emotional pain led me to be a clinical social worker. By my junior year of college, I knew that my work would be in the mental health field. Little did I know that I suffered from unworthiness, shame, and significant anxiety and that one motive underlying my career choice was the desire to help myself.

I begin by sharing about my upbringing so that you know I, too, walk this healing path. I was raised in a family of eight children in rural Iowa. My father came from a large, working-class family and was a farm laborer. We got by with the help of food commodities, county relief funds, and hand-me-down clothes. My father was a hard-to-know, passive man and a child molester who was adept at convincing us that what he did was our little secret. He sexually abused me and some of my sisters. He also molested a few grandchildren and at least one neighbor's daughter.

My mother was overwhelmed, shunned by my father's family, and not supported much by her own family. She probably had attention deficit disorder, as organization and task completion were difficult for her. Our home was messy and unsanitary, making it too embarrassing to invite friends over. As I was her oldest daughter, she relied on me, and I learned how to over function. Somehow, she finished her B.A., and by the time I was in high school, she had a job teaching special needs children. In many ways, she parented well. When I was young, she sang happy songs and danced with me. When I was a teenager, she insisted that I have a better life, hold my head high, go to college, and kick a man in the balls if I needed to protect myself.

I took an anxiety screening instrument while in graduate school and received the highest anxiety score in the class. Not knowing I was anxious, I felt mortified and surprised that others didn't feel like I did. That score left me wondering if I was different from others and how I could be considered anxious when I felt normal. I was also curious about what it would be like to be relaxed when talking in a group.

It does not serve you for me to detail my entire healing journey. I will tell you that I literally practice everything I am going to teach you. As a result, I suffer much less in the same old ways and I truly love myself. I am still amazed about my good fortune.

At times, I trip up and slide back into old patterns. I have learned to rely on the resources that I teach in this workbook. In fact, as I wrote this manuscript, I called on them in the middle of the night when old patterns arose. But, I am getting ahead of myself! More about this leg of my personal journey in the conclusion.

Healing is not a magic pill that you take. It is a way of living a day at a time, with unfolding insights and capacities, until healing becomes a journey for which you are grateful.

This workbook is the culmination of my professional knowledge to date. My patients would tell you that they credit much of their healing to the evidenced-based mindfulness approaches that fill these pages. I share clinical stories in the "Notes to Clinician" section at the beginning of each chapter, which is relevant for clinicians and non-clinicians alike to read, as it will help you connect to this material.

This workbook is deeply rooted in clinical research. I reference studies throughout the text so that you know how grounded in research this approach is. Additionally, recent brain science findings substantiate and explain the benefits of mindfulness.

As you read, you will understand that you really can make significant changes in how your brain functions! This is so useful that I begin the workbook with a cursory look at the brain. You don't have to love science to enjoy this material. It is easy to digest and will help you understand yourself more clearly.

Even if you feel stuck, I assure you that you can make changes. You can reduce emotional pain, including that which has persisted. Healing does require some personal responsibility, but a little effort can reap big results. The incredible human brain, including yours, is influenceable and thus trainable.

Healing is not burdensome, although it is intentional. The old saying about doing "the same ole thing" and expecting different results applies here. This workbook is about you rolling up your sleeves and making efforts for your own wellbeing. The practices are enjoyable and easy to do and train your brain to serve you better. They teach you to focus on the present moment, concentrate on what is most helpful, treat yourself with kindness, gently care for your emotional pain, and cultivate contentment in daily life.

I emphasize that these are pleasant practices. Here is an analogy: Showering your body, washing your hair, brushing your teeth, and wearing clean clothes keep your body healthy, add to your comfort, and invite others to be close. Plus, your daily hygiene ritual is usually enjoyable, especially if you don't rush. Practicing mindfulness, yoga, and kindness is daily hygiene for your overall wellbeing. And when done consistently, these practices literally make brain changes that impart happiness.

You don't have to have a diagnosis of depression or anxiety to benefit from this workbook. However, most everyone is diagnosable at some point in life, at least temporarily, in response to high stresses and inevitable, painful losses. After all, we are vulnerable beings who feel deeply. Fortunately, we also have tremendous resilience and can bounce back from adversity.

Some people may have a genetic predisposition for depression and anxiety. If that is the case for you, know that you are not to blame and you are not alone. No one selects a biological susceptibility for mood distress any more than anyone signs up for an Alzheimer gene. Additionally, the field of epigenetics has shown that family and circumstances greatly influence which genes are silenced and expressed. I want to stress the significance of family and community on the developing brain to help you appreciate the power of this socialization.

The likelihood of your optimal genetic potential being "turned on" or manifested is dramatically affected in early life by how you were parented and what was going on in the culture around you. Just imagine being raised in a war-torn country in the midst of fear, bombs, and lack of basic provisions. Your sense of who you are, how safe the world is, and what the future holds in store expresses, at least partially, what you experienced. Who you are today is just one of many possible yous. If you had you been raised elsewhere, you would be another expression of you.

Whatever did and didn't happen at home and in your community shaped you. History is history, and biology is biology. However, thanks to the trainable brain, how you are today does not have to be the end of the story. Now, it is up to you. Become informed and choose healing.

I wrote this workbook in a self-help, first person style to support you step by step on your transformational journey, possibly in conjunction with a health care provider who can counsel you along the way. To make this a valuable treatment resource, I conclude these introductory comments with a section for mental health professionals to explain how to use this workbook.

Introduction for Mental Health Professionals

Mindfulness approaches and brain knowledge go hand in hand. Some understanding of both improves your treatment outcomes and makes this work deeply fulfilling. Together, they have transformed my professional work, much to the benefit of the people with whom I work.

In my current practice, I teach my patients to do the following:

- Observe their thoughts
- Soothe their dysregulated nervous systems
- Care for their minds and bodies
- Approach feelings with mercy
- Focus on life-affirming thoughts
- Stay in the present moment
- Enjoy the goodness of life

Thanks to mindfulness, my patients' minds and bodies become healthier. We often enjoy our time together, and many say, as their moods calm and lift and unworthiness loses its grip, that what helps them the most is learning to be kind to themselves.

You have heard some patients report that self-affirmations don't provide benefit or relief. This is not because these patients don't want change. Most likely, it is because their nervous systems do not resonate with positive thoughts. Positive self-talk can be like telling yourself that your thumb doesn't hurt after accidently hitting it with a hammer. Your body simply doesn't believe your words. In reality, nervous system dysregulation, unconscious attitudes, emotional motivations, and protective movement patterns remain powerful forces when psychological distress stems from trauma. Therefore, it is essential to be knowledgeable about the impact of trauma on the brain and nervous system and about how to bring mindfulness of body and emotions as well as thoughts into treatment.

The miracle of mindfulness is that it helps you recognize old habitual thoughts, emotions, and behaviors; to accept yourself; and to make positive changes. But that is not all. Perhaps most importantly, you learn to be a good friend to yourself. Teach these skills to your patients, and you give them a gift of a lifetime.

I begin each section with a "Benefits & Clinician Notes" that explains the relevance for and application of the material into your clinical treatment. The workbook is written in a self-help style to reinforce your therapy interventions. You can easily recommend sections as homework to be discussed in follow-up sessions.

I hope that you become inspired to practice for your benefit and the benefit of those with whom you work. None of us are immune to suffering, and we deserve healing, too. Mindfulness and self-compassion become more powerful clinical resources when you practice them yourself. Then, your recommendations arise out of lived experience, and your kind presence becomes a healing force.

CHAPTER 1

Neuroscience & Psychoeducation

Benefits & Clinician Notes

✓ A significant reduction in the self-blame that so often accompanies depression, anxiety, and shame

✓ Psychoeducation that increases understanding about inner life

✓ The "turning on" of the thinking brain and calming of the lower brain centers

✓ Teaching on how to selectively focus in ways that empower and encourage

Use this chapter to educate your patients about how their brains function and to reassure them that they can help themselves. Knowledge is power, and utilizing this information as psychoeducation helps your patients understand why they are the way they are. It also demonstrates that your patients' efforts will make a difference. This information instills possibility and increases motivation for doing the work that needs to be done.

I want to underscore the therapeutic value of talking about the brain with patients with an example. Susan (not her real name), a lovely middle-age woman with chronic depression, learned that her historical way of coping with stress by having suicidal thoughts was probably inevitable. Her father said that he wished she were dead and threatened to kill her on multiple occasions when she was a girl. A discussion about interpersonal neurobiology, detailed in this chapter, gave her insight as to the origin of those thoughts. She realized that suicidal ideation was a trauma memory with its roots in childhood rather than a current desire on which to be acted. She practiced naming suicidal wishes as "old trauma memories." That little bit of brain information gave her hope, and over time she began to focus on improving the quality of her life.

The way your brain processes information is the result of some mixture of genetics and interaction with the world around you. The brain is complex and involves much more than thoughts. However, even the thoughts that pass through your mind express your intricate relationship with the outer world. The negative thoughts of depression, including the wish to "not be " and the painful belief that you are "not okay," and the fearful worries of anxiety are not manifest in a newborn.

Stress to your patients that they learned to think the way they do. With the help of the practices that follow, they can discover where their thoughts come from, cultivate healthy ways to relate to thoughts, and fill their minds with thoughts that support happiness.

This chapter is more informational and less practice oriented than the others. It begins with a teaching on neuroplasticity that explains how adaptive and trainable the human brain is. The rest of the chapter offers simple, useful ways to understand and enhance brain functioning.

Neuroplasticity—Your Brain's Ability to Organize and Learn

A human brain organizes itself rapidly in infancy and early childhood in response to the outer world. Some say a child's brain is like a sponge that soaks up information from the environment around it. How this learning occurs is interesting. The brain reorganizes by forming new neural connections. Specifically, what changes is the strength of connections between actively engaged neurons. Not surprisingly, the strength increases when experience is emotionally charged and also when it is frequently repeated.

Neural connections become embedded, for better or worse, as habits that carry on outside of awareness, or unconsciously. For example, you don't think about how to tie shoelaces or say hello to friends—you just do it. Additionally, neural connections make conscious learning possible, such as when you painstakingly learn computer software programs, no matter how old you are.

Your adult brain is not static, even though it is patterned. It continues to detect and respond to life as it occurs inside of and around you. Even small changes in life circumstances, behaviors, thoughts, and emotions affect your brain, causing it to reorganize. There may be brain changes with aging that require you to be more intentional when learning some new skills. However, throughout your life, you can enhance your brain's plasticity with focused attention, determination, hard work, and a lifestyle that includes healthy nutrition, exercise, and friendships. Overall, this information is encouraging and lets you know that your efforts to change make a positive difference.

It is important to note that the human brain is both vulnerable and resilient. As Michael Merzenich (2013) teaches, it is just as easy to generate negative changes as it is positive ones. Obviously, you want to establish neural connections that ease anxiety, lessen depression, and turn around low self-worth. Let's say you want to learn to be kind to yourself. One helpful skill is singing when you are distressed. To make a habit of singing, repeat a comforting tune a hundred times, and over time, the neurons engaged will develop vigorous connections.

Learning is interpersonal because the human brain is a social organism. I want to emphasize this reality. You were not born with language, religion, or defined gender roles. These beliefs were put into you during childhood and were later adopted and/or rejected by you. You heard countless times the words that became your primary language. You may have accompanied your parents to their place of worship, where you were indoctrinated in their religious beliefs. As if by osmosis, you learned what it is to be a man, a woman or a nonbinary gender according to what your caretakers modeled and how they were treated at home and in the surrounding culture.

Likewise, you were not born with low or high self-worth. Unworthiness, if it arose during childhood, was implanted via interpersonal relationships. Your young brain learned what it was repeatedly exposed to. It picked up what you heard and saw.

Fortunately, learning is not static. You are not doomed to live out your years with the brain organization that came with you into adult life. With a little bit of information, some motivation, and a small time commitment, you can reduce old painful patterns and teach your brain in the ways of compassion, ease, optimism, and the innate value of human life.

Get ready to learn and repeat practices that will change your brain and your life in positive ways.

Practice ···

Personal Example of Neuroplasticity

Journal a personal example of neuroplasticity. Name a seemingly innocent thought—not one that distresses you—that you repeated and later discovered was not true. Where did that thought come from? Who else believed this? For example, as a teenager I believed that it was wise to "keep a stiff upper lip," which meant to not let emotions show. That conviction was passed down to me by both grandmothers; however, I later learned that this belief need not apply to my life.

_____

_____

_____

Creating Healthy Neuronal Connections

Experience how your brain learns as it establishes new neural pathways in response to changes in your behavior and thoughts, especially when you are in a pleasant, safe environment.

Practice ·····································

Experiencing How Your Brain Learns

This three-part practice calms your nervous system, focuses your attention, and cultivates a compassionate relationship with yourself.

- First, sit comfortably in a quiet setting.
- Breathe in and bring your hands to your heart. Breathe out and bring your hands to your lap. Slowly repeat several times.
- Sit with your folded hands by your chest to quietly center. Close your eyes and focus on your heart.
- Repeat these words: "I am learning to take care of myself."

The above yoga and breathing sequence is an introductory practice to beneficial self-care that trains your brain in the ways of calmness and kindness.

Optimal Conditions for Neuroplasticity

You can create optimal conditions for neuroplasticity to quicken learning. To make positive changes, do the following. Select your desired outcome, visualize what you want, and intentionally take action, as the following mini-practice of soothing self-talk demonstrates.

Practice ·····································

Creating Optimal Conditions for Neuroplasticity

Begin with stating your desired outcome, which in this example is cultivating reassuring self-talk. Now add a visualization—literally see an image of you encouraging yourself the way a close friend would. Find your comforting voice. If needed, first see yourself talking kindly to someone else to help you access tenderness. Finally, add intentional action, which in this case is speaking to yourself. Say "In this moment, I am okay," "One step at a time," "Have a little faith," or another thought that soothes.

Notice the effects of doing this. You may feel more centered, calmer. You created an intentional experience of soothing self-talk that was neither habitual nor reflexive.

The Triune Brain

One way to look at your remarkable brain is to divide it into three regions that are referred to as **old brain, midbrain**, and **new brain**. This, the triune brain model, looks at the brain as it evolved from reptiles to mammals to humans. It shows brain structures and describes their functions. Although the terminology may imply that the old brain, midbrain, and new brain are independently operating regions, this is not the case. Neuroscientist Barbara Finlay (with colleague Uchiyama) reported that it is inaccurate to conceive of brain evolution as resulting in independently operating brain regions that were stacked on top of each other (2015). She states that these brain divisions are present in all vertebrates and that the brain evolved through reorganization as it expanded. Thus, the brain systems discussed in the following sections are interdependent and mutually reinforcing. When one part of the brain is affected, so are the others.

Brain science is young, and what we understand about human brain functioning continues to change. Still, some rudimentary understanding of the brain offers perspective that informs treatment approaches.

Here is a brief introduction to this model: The old brain is referred to as the **reptilian system**. This cluster of brain structures primarily pertains to instinct, territoriality, and survival. The midbrain is referred to as the **limbic system**. Its structures mostly pertain to survival, emotions, and the capacity to feel connected and contented. The new brain, or **neocortex**, is the most highly developed in humans. It mainly pertains to capacity for analysis and is the home of concentration, intention, and choice. Remember, these brain regions work together.

Reptilian Brain, or Hindbrain—Known as the Area of the Autonomic Nervous System

The reptilian brain is mostly instinctual. It governs vital organ functioning and physical survival. This unconscious brain region regulates heart rate, breathing, digestion, and more. Injury to the brain stem threatens vital organ functioning and the survival of the body.

The hindbrain is the home of the autonomic nervous system, which consists of two main branches, the sympathetic and parasympathetic. The sympathetic branch is the emergency system that puts your body in an alarm response of fight, flight, freeze/feigning dead when your brain detects threat. It does so by increasing your heart rate and sending oxygen-rich blood to your muscles to prepare for life-saving action.

The parasympathetic branch is the "rest, relax, and digest" system. When your brain no longer senses danger, it slows heart rate, deepens breath, and relaxes muscles. This enables you to sleep, digest food, think clearly, learn more easily, and experience contentment and pleasure.

Many people suffer from an overly active sympathetic branch. According to Bessel van der Kolk and colleagues (2014), two thirds of people who have been traumatized live with increased adrenal activity and associated anxiety. Consequently, they remain frightened and/or angry for a longer time following a trigger or even most of the time, whether they are aware of it or not. In fact, a hallmark indicator of post-traumatic stress disorder (PTSD) is racing heart. In other words, if you suffer from chronic anxiety, you may well have a dysregulated autonomic nervous system.

A racing heart and other anxiety/PTSD symptoms means that your relaxation response is not optimally activated. If that is true for you, it is essential to your wellbeing that you find a way to turn on your parasympathetic branch. One way to relax is with yoga. According to the September 2017 *Harvard Mental Health Newsletter,* hatha yoga, which combines breathing practices, postures, and deep rest, increases your body's ability to respond to stress more flexibly.

Limbic Brain or Mid Brain—Known as the Area of Emotions

The limbic system, or midbrain, is instinctual. This brain region is further evolved in animals than in reptiles. Reptiles are more independent at birth. Newborn animals are not self-sufficient and rely on their herd, parents, or at least the mother, for protection, food, grooming, and emotional bonding.

The main structures in this region are the hippocampus, amygdala, and hypothalamus. I discuss each separately. However, remember that the brain is complex and its structures function in relationship with each other.

The **hippocampus** is involved in storing long-term memory and has many receptors for cortisol, the stress hormone. When your body is flooded with cortisol, your ability to learn and remember is impaired. This partially explains why stress and anxiety compromise school performance in students.

The **amygdala** is highly involved with emotions, survival instincts, and memory. Your amygdala remembers past events, and if it senses a new threat, real or not, it indirectly initiates the fight, flight, freeze/feign dead response. Its detection of and response to perceived threat occur unconsciously, thus not intentionally. According to Frewen and Lanius (2015), when young children are maltreated, their amygdalae may become enlarged and perceive danger where there is none.

The **hypothalamus** keeps the body in a regulated, normal state. Signals from the body sent to the brain let the hypothalamus know if balance is being achieved. For example, when your hypothalamus receives information that the body is too hot, it tells the body to sweat. It plays an essential function in emotions. It secrets oxytocin, the bonding, or "love," hormone released during nursing, sex, and romance. Oxytocin has been dubbed the "cuddle chemical." The hypothalamus also works with the pituitary gland to influence the endocrine system, including the adrenal glands that initiate the fight, flight, freeze/feign dead response.

Your hypothalamus detects threatening stimulation and triggers the stress response of the autonomic nervous system. It reacts to sensory input of real threat, such as a bolt of lightning when you are on a mountain hiking on a trail above the tree line. It also responds to negative thinking and emotional distress. You can literally think and feel yourself into a heightened state of alarm when all is calm in your outer world.

Your emotions are constructed as a result of what your brain perceives from inside the body as well as from the outer world. In fact, recent research by Lisa Feldman (2017) challenges the science that says human emotion is universal and a result of a distinct and primitive brain region. Their work suggests that you individually create emotions through a complex process that includes your thoughts.

It is obvious that your brain takes in information through sensory perception. It is less obvious that it perceives the condition of your body as well. It picks up sensations, especially those produced within the gut and other internal organs, through a process called interoception. This internally gathered data is also detected by the hypothalamus. If your body's data suggest disturbance, the hypothalamus, working with the pituitary gland, sends a wake-up call to the adrenal glands.

To sum it up, information from both inner body and outer world are perceived by your unconscious brain and interpreted according to past experience. Now, add in your thinking brain, which categorizes what is perceived and reacts according to what it believes. Together, your body experiences and your mind conceptualizations to construct emotions. No wonder emotions persist and escalate. Mind and body mutually reinforce them!

Here is encouraging news: Mindfulness practices are medicine for the middle brain. You can become more aware of what is happening in the body and train the nervous system to relax and reduce false interpretations of threat. According to Bessel van der Kolk and associates (2014), yoga increases awareness of internal bodily sensations and also activates the parasympathetic relaxation response. Additionally, a collection of research by Desbordes and colleagues (2012) shows that mindfulness practices can reduce amygdala reactivity to emotional stimulation.

Neomammalian Brain or Neocortex—Known as the Area of Advanced Thinking

The neocortex is the cluster of brain structures involved in advanced thinking. The prefrontal cortex, part of the neocortex, is located at very front of your brain, above and behind the eyebrows. It is involved in your capacity to be intentional, make choices, reason through decisions, generate symbolic thought, observe thoughts, be self-reflective, and regulate emotions rather than react to them.

The prefrontal cortex is most evolved in humans—just compare the prefrontal lobes of humans with those of cats and dogs. According to Joe Dispenza (2007), the prefrontal lobe of a cat comprises about 3 percent of its cerebral cortex. The prefrontal lobe of a dog comprises about 7 percent of its cerebral cortex. Dogs are more trainable. Dogs, not cats, assist police and military and aid visually impaired individuals. It's also more common for dogs, rather than cats, to be used for comforting people in nursing homes and providing companionship to people with PTSD. The prefrontal lobe of the human brain comprises anywhere from 25 to 35 percent of its cerebral cortex. This suggests that you are quite trainable!

This part of your brain does not reach maturity until you are in your mid-twenties. It is influenced by experience, including childhood maltreatment (Frewen & Lanius, 2015). Childhood experiences, for better or worse, affected your ability to focus, concentrate, make healthy decisions, and manage your impulses.

You are not doomed to live your years with the brain that came with you into adulthood. Your brain grows new grey matter and creates new neuronal pathways throughout life. Work with the prefrontal lobes and you alter brain functioning, because these lobes are densely connected via neurons to the rest of your brain.

Your Brain and Emotions

This section describes the three emotional motivation systems. It also explains how emotions guide actions and inform attitudes. This information prepares you to approach your emotional life with the practices described later in the workbook.

The first emotional motivation system is your threat response system. Your brain's main job is to preserve your life. It relies on your fight, flight, freeze/feign dead response as its first responder to risky or alarming situations. As you read in the section on the limbic system, the perception of danger depends on communication among the amygdala, hypothalamus, and thought processes. Threat is detected, and the next thing you know, your body is in a state of alarm. In preparation for action, your heart pounds, your breath becomes shallow, and your muscles tense.

However, according to Lanius (2015), in the aftermath of childhood maltreatment, this part of your brain can perceive danger where there is none. As a result, your sympathetic nervous system remains activated, as if threat is ever present. Considering how shockingly prevalent trauma in childhood is, it's no wonder that many of us feel revved up and frightened much of the time.

The second system is your affiliation system. Your brain's survival depends on association with others. Throughout life, your brain is dramatically influenced by the people you surround yourself with. This is so true that Daniel Siegel (2010) defined the human brain as a social organism and coined the term *interpersonal neurobiology* to reflect how interactive with others your brain is. You are not nearly as autonomous or independent as you might like to think.

Your brain is designed to be comforted by others during times of duress. When you are upset and scared, you naturally gravitate toward people who are kind, when possible. Gentle touch and caring words lower your stress response by activating your parasympathetic relaxation response.

Research confirms that contact with friends and supportive family provides the sense of belonging that allows you to feel calmer. Tuija Turunen (2014) found that children with secure attachment, meaning they have a close emotional bond to parents, suffer fewer PTSD symptoms after traumatic incidents such as school shootings. And, undeniably, children and adults who have loving support systems enjoy better physical and mental health.

Your ability to emotionally attach to others is initially developed by having a safe, loving bond with parents during early childhood. Children who feel protected by parents learn that closeness with others soothes. They develop a secure attachment style and go on to trust and rely on others.

Relationships provide stability unless people who were supposed to be there were inconsistent, hurt you, or in other ways significantly betrayed you. Sadly, under those conditions, an insecure or avoidant attachment style can result—the person may require a lot of reassurance from others or find it difficult to sustain closeness with others. As a result, their adult relationships may suffer. Statistics vary but suggest that approximately 55 percent of adults have secure attachment styles. Moullin and associates (2014) found that 40 percent of U.S. children have insecure attachment style. Mindfulness and self-compassion practices help you repair that breach of bonding and enable you to seek and tolerate support from safe people.

Third is your drive system. Your brain requires stimulation and is on the lookout for something to explore. This is a biological need. Doing so gives you a sense of vitality and mastery. Children play and study in order to learn about the world around them. Teenagers practice driving, explore dating skills, and develop decision making to expand their capabilities. Adults learn how to earn money, take care of home and family, make sense of life, and find meaning.

Human brains, including yours, are novelty seekers. According to Folletto, Hopper, and colleagues (2015), our "seeking circuitry" is what provides the drive to intentionally pursue anything. The issue is *what* you pursue, not *if* you pursue. These authors theorize that in the aftermath of trauma, when the threat system remains overactive, this brain circuitry turns toward safety and control. The risk of making mistakes, being emotionally vulnerable, asking for help, or trying something new may be too daunting. Life may shrink and the world become smaller, even dull, although predictable.

Primary Emotional Motivators

Gilbert and Chodon (2014) teach that the three emotional systems are primary motivators that guide your actions and inform your attitudes. They are not intentional choices—they are unconscious, powerful responses of a brain designed to keep you alive. You can become educated and more conscious about them. Doing so makes it possible for you to lovingly care for them so you can act on desired motives.

How these systems function today is informed by the past. Consider what prior trauma does. It can cause your fear system to go into overdrive and misinterpret life as dangerous, based on previous threats. Trauma can cause your affiliation system to not trust others, based on former betrayals. It can cause your drive system to seek safety and control, based on earlier deprivation. You can see how the past influences the present and at times is almost recreated in it.

You, like many people, may have a predictable response to real and perceived threat. Depending on how your nervous system responded in the past, you may automatically react to threat with anger, fear, or immobilization. Following is some detail to make this clear.

If you are prone to anger, you are apt to come across as irritated, argumentative, challenging, aggressive, or blaming. If you are fearful, you may show up as anxious, conflict avoidant, averse to risks, people pleasing, or needing to appear in control. If you go into a freeze and feign dead response, you may experience confusion, numbing out, difficulty responding, feeling different from others, or wanting to hide. You may know all three. None is right or superior—these reactions are self-protective and unconscious.

Practice ···

Inquiry into Your Emotional Motivation Systems

Inquiry is an investigation, an effort to seek understanding, and a way to become conscious. Use the following questions to prompt your examination.

Threat System:

When stressed, do you typically respond with anger, fear, or numbing out?

_____

_____

_____

_____

What happens to your heart rate and breath?

_____

_____

_____

_____

Are you easily startled? When?

_____

_____

_____

_____

Do you generally perceive the world as dangerous? Why?

_____

_____

_____

_____

Do you carry chronic muscular tension? If so, where?

_____

_____

_____

_____

Why/how did your body learn to react to stress the way it does? Perhaps describe an early memory of being stressed/frightened.

_____

_____

_____

_____

Affiliation System:

Are you secretive about your emotional distress? How did you learn this?

_____

_____

_____

_____

Are you a lone soldier? When? Why?

_____

_____

_____

_____

Do you seek support from others? How?

_____

_____

_____

_____

Do you rely "too much" on others and have difficulty soothing yourself? Why?

_____

_____

_____

_____

Is it hard for you to be alone? Why?

_____

_____

_____

_____

Do you let yourself be vulnerable with others? When?

_____

_____

_____

_____

Do you believe that people will be there for you? Based on what?

_____

_____

_____

_____

Do you attempt to control others? Why?

_____

_____

_____

_____

How/why did you learn to relate to others when you are stressed?

_____

_____

_____

_____

Drive System:

Do you seek change frequently? Why?

_____

_____

_____

_____

Do you prefer a lifestyle of conformity and "fitting in?" Based on what?

_____

_____

_____

_____

Does desire for safety inhibit your willingness to learn new tasks, assert your preferences, show vulnerability to others?

_____

_____

_____

_____

Do you seek adrenaline thrills and/or take physically risky challenges?

_____

_____

_____

_____

Do you seek novelty?

_____

_____

_____

Do you avoid opportunities to advance your career?

_____

_____

_____

_____

Do you push beyond your limits and/or take pride in being "the best?"

_____

_____

_____

_____

Do you seek perfectionism and being in control? How does that affect you?

_____

_____

_____

_____

How/why did the seekers of your brain learn to respond in the way they do?

_____

_____

_____

_____

Negativity Bias of Your Brain

It is worth repeating that your brain is all about keeping you alive. Accordingly, your brain is designed to notice danger, and thus focus on the negative, so that it can prepare your body for self-defense. To accomplish this, it remains on alert to detect what it perceives as threatening events in the outer world.

Thanks to your brain's survival orientation, your hypothalamus also reacts to scary and negative ideas. Thoughts such as, "Plans never work out for me," "What if I can't do it?" "There is something wrong with me," and "Nobody understands me" trigger a fight, flight, freeze/ feign dead response. A vicious cycle ensues. Your body being revved up validates to your mind that there must be something to be upset about, and on it goes—body and mind constructing personal reality.

To emphasize the magnitude of this survival imperative, Rick Hanson (2009) coined the following phrase: "Negativity sticks to the brain like Velcro, and positivity slides off like Teflon." He also teaches that you can use the intentionality of your prefrontal cortex to interrupt this cycle.

Hanson (2009) and Davidson and Begley (2012) explain that you need to pause and savor goodness, to literally take more time with thoughts that uplift and inspire. One way to accomplish this is by intentionally recalling life-enhancing experiences with others. Teach your brain to focus on and remember goodness, and you will have a more relaxed body and a more balanced perspective on the way life is.

Practice ···

Positive Memories

In the space following, list several memories that correspond to each question. Give yourself time. It can take gentle effort to let these kinds of memories arise, considering the mind's habit of focusing on what is wrong. Simple examples are powerful. What comes to mind does not need to be dramatic.

Recall someone seeing the good in you. Describe how that acknowledgement impacted you.

_____

_____

_____

Recall someone who showed compassion to you when you were sad or felt vulnerable.

_____

_____

_____

Recall a time when someone unexpectedly helped or supported you.

_____

_____

_____

Recall a time when someone took the time to thank you for something you did.

_____

_____

_____

Recall a time when a stranger extended a small act of kindness to you.

_____

_____

_____

Recall when someone telephoned or texted you and made your day.

_____

_____

_____

Practice ···

Savoring the Good

It is not enough to recall goodness. Hanson (2009) and Davidson and Begley (2012) advocate soaking in positive events so they stick in your emotional memory. To intensify such memories, take another step. Visualize a golden light or warm liquid to draw the experience of goodness into your heart. Let it sink in. Hold it there for several seconds so that it is both a cognitive and emotional remembrance.

Select one of the recalled positive associations with others from the previous "Practice" section. Pause, intensify it, and using your active imagination, let it sink into your heart. Savor and enjoy.

Notice the effect this practice had on your body, emotions, and outlook. Write about your experience in the following spaces.

_____

_____

_____

You Are Not Alone—Your Ancestors Are with You

Ancestors dramatically influence your identity. Even the name with which you identity was most likely given by an ancestor (e.g., parent). A brief consideration makes this clear. Envision who you would be if you had been born into royalty in Saudi Arabia. Now, imagine what you would be like if you were raised as a member of the lowest caste in India. Add another dimension—picture the dissimilar outcome in either circumstance if your family was filled with love and laughter or if it was filled with anger and neglect.

You do not have to look deep to appreciate how family circumstances affected you or look far to see how family lives on in you. You survived infancy, so you were provided for. People were there for you during your formative years, perhaps even some you have forgotten. Sadly, you may also have been mistreated. In a landmark study, Felitti and colleagues (1998) reported that more than half of children in the United States experience maltreatment during childhood.

This next practice is designed to assist you in calling on ancestors as resources for you. You can selectively nurture the beneficial ways in which family and community shaped your personality. To prompt you, here is an example of a favorable ancestral influence: My mother consistently said, "Hold your head up—you are as important as others." When I feel insecure in front of an audience, I stand a little taller and smile softly. I feel her in me even though she died a few years ago.

Be gentle with the following practice. If thinking about a particular person causes distress, move on to another one. If appropriate, revisit the first person you thought of and see if they had some beneficial impact. Most people are not totally good or bad. Even people who cared for you made mistakes. When a relationship has caused enough damage, memory can crystallize on the negative. Remarkably, over time, you may be able to recall a positive characteristic, even if it is something small, about that person. For example, my father mistreated me and my sisters. He also enjoyed the outdoors, as do I. My husband and I have long lived out in the country, and I love taking walks on our rural property.

Practice ···

Listing Beneficial Impacts of Ancestors

Name the beneficial strengths, qualities, attitudes, and behaviors that characterize the following persons. When needed, call on them as resources. Remember, you are never alone.

Mother or mother figure:

_____

_____

_____

Father or father figure:

_____

_____

_____

Grandparents:

_____

_____

_____

Aunts, uncles, and extended family:

_____

_____

_____

Secular and religious teachers:

_____

_____

_____

Neighbors and others:

_____

_____

_____

Default Mode Network of the Brain

When you are awake and not focused on the outside world, your mind goes into drifting and repetitive thoughts. Buckner and colleagues (2008) named these wandering thoughts "the default mode network" because these thoughts occur "by default" when you are not paying attention. In Eastern philosophy, these thoughts, which roam forward to the future, back to the past, and into ideas about yourself and others, are called "the monkey mind." Compare these thoughts to a monkey aimlessly swinging from branch to branch to conjure up a picture of how this works. Alternatively, consider these thoughts as coming from your undirected mind.

Your prefrontal lobes focus attention according to your direction. Other times, attention is unguided, and next thing you know, you are lost in thought. Your mind cannot be focused and unfocused simultaneously.

Default mode network thoughts have four pathways on which to travel: the past, the future, the story of "me and my life," and analysis/comparison. You know them as the thought trails of rumination, anticipation, personal life concerns, and comparison and judgment. The pathways cross and merge, yet your default mode network may have a most frequently trod course. You studied how the brain gravitates toward negativity, so you can understand the tendency for these thoughts to drift toward problems and concerns.

Repeated thoughts become habitual—that is just the way it is, thanks to neuroplasticity. There is no need to blame yourself. Become familiar with the pathway(s) most traveled by your default mode network thoughts. Over time, you can catch thoughts when they start down the road(s) of suffering and choose to walk on new pathways. You will learn how to cultivate life-enhancing thoughts in Chapter 4.

Be gentle with this next practice so that you don't collapse into self-criticism.

Practice ··

Frequently Occurring Thoughts of Your "Default Mode Network"

The past (ruminating about mistakes, celebrating previous successes, reviewing grievances, regrets, remembering loved ones, recalling good times, longing for good old days, rehashing events).

_____

_____

_____

_____

The future (fears, hopeful anticipations, worries about events/people, day dreams, fantasies).

_____

_____

_____

_____

The story of you (typical adjectives/phrases that you use to describe yourself, such as *helpful, smart, stupid, lazy, ambitious, caring, lovable, not lovable, enough, not good enough, healthy, sickly*).

_____

_____

_____

_____

The story of your life (attitudes and perspectives about life, such as "Things do/do not usually work out for me," "You generally can/can't trust others," "Life is often hard/easy," "Others do/don't understand me," thoughts about being a victim/blaming others, pessimism/optimism).

_____

_____

_____

_____

Analysis and comparison (critical thoughts directed at self and or others, judging self/others as superior/inferior, viewing events as good or bad, perfectionistic expectations).

_____

_____

_____

_____

CHAPTER 2

Mindfulness Foundation

Benefits & Clinician Notes

✓ A basic understanding of concepts that are utilized throughout the remaining chapters

✓ Experience with introductory mindfulness skills

✓ Increased knowledge of awareness

✓ Exploration of awareness of body, thoughts, and sensory input

✓ "Trying on" of meditative practices

I want to sing praises to the power of mindfulness. The foundation of transformation, it helps you create neuropathways of emotional relief, self-compassion, and happiness. Mindfulness anchors your awareness in the present moment, which calms your threat system, engages your thinking brain, and kicks in your capacity to choose. Mindfulness practices teach you to approach painful emotions with loving kindness and to focus your attention on what is healthy and enjoyable.

Mindfulness comprises two core capacities: the ability to choose what to focus on and the ability to be aware of what is going on. These two capacities rely on each other as closely as do the palm and the back of the hand. Together, they help you to lovingly take care of, rather than being lost in, inner life. Equally important, these two capacities lead to contentment (see Chapter 8). The result is a significant decrease in symptomology, an increase in emotional and mental resiliency, and a delightful increase in the ability to enjoy the miracle of life.

This brief clinical example highlights using observing and concentrating for patient relief. John (not his real name) had long struggled with self-blame and regret. After spending years in various therapies, he had insight about himself, yet his low mood persisted. He decided to try a mindfulness approach and sought treatment with me. I introduced him to meditation and referred him to an ongoing meditation class. I stressed the importance of learning to observe thoughts rather than remain lost in them and to concentrate on breathing when thoughts drifted to the past and self-recrimination.

Here is more of what John discovered. When he was lost in a painful rumination, his present moment consisted of reliving the past. He was disempowered and unaware of spinning off in a thought-generated experience. By observing thoughts in a regular meditation practice, he became more aware throughout the day of when his thoughts drifted backwards in time. John liked to say "Wow, I did it again" to come back to the present moment. Next, he intentionally felt his feet on the floor and took a deep breath to anchor himself in the here and now.

John learned to focus on thoughts and behaviors that are life enhancing. At the end of our work together, he said that the most helpful skill he learned is to watch thoughts rather than process or chase after them. He also agreed that daily meditation is one of the best things he can do for his mood.

Mindfulness Definition and Basic Types

Mindfulness, usually defined as "nonjudgmental awareness of what is occurring in present-moment experience," has two primary forms, concentration practice and observing practice.

In **concentration practice,** you select some specific object of focus, such as breath or other bodily sensation (e.g., thumbs pressing index fingers) or a sacred word, and intend to keep your attention there. This is a single-pointed focus practice. The primary intention is to concentrate. When you discover attention has wandered, usually into thought, gently refocus on your breath, other chosen bodily sensation, or sacred word. This practice increases mental concentration, relaxes the physical body, quiets the mind, and helps to regulate emotional distress.

In **observation practice,** you select a focal point, such as breath or a sacred word, on which you can redirect your attention after it gets lost in thoughts or strong physical sensations. This is a wider-lens focus practice. The primary purpose is to observe so that you can see, sense, and discover what goes on in your inner experience. You, as awareness, watch thoughts come and go. You, as awareness, pull back when attention becomes ensnared in thoughts, because, once caught by thoughts, you are less able to observe. You pull back by redirecting attention to breath or sacred word to restore your capacity to watch. This practice reveals the contents of your thoughts to you. It also calms and quiets your mind.

Concentration and observation work like the palm and back of your hand—they are inextricably joined together. In any mindfulness practice, it is helpful to first establish stability by concentrating your mind. If you continue on with an observing practice, you then expand, even soften, your observational field to include your present-moment experience. This way, you as awareness learn about your interior life of thoughts, emotions, and physical sensations.

Practices ·

Concentration and Observation

Five-Minute Concentration Practice Sit in a comfortable upright position. Set a timer for 5 minutes. Place your hands on your lap. Pay attention to breathing. Notice breath coming in and breath going out. Notice the complete in breath and the complete out breath. When attention drifts, refocus on breathing.

Five-Minute Observation Practice—Start with Concentration and Expand Awareness Continue sitting. Set a timer for another 5 minutes. Open your eyes and slowly scan the room around you, looking and seeing, for a few seconds as an experience of noticing the outer world. Now close your eyes to tune into your inner world. Sense physical sensations, watch thoughts come and go, notice whatever you notice on the inside. If attention gravitates to thinking or is otherwise distracted, gently refocus on breathing until your mind is quiet and stable. Then begin expanding your lens and observe life in your interior.

Commentary on the Practice As you experienced, mindfulness includes both concentrating and noticing as essential skills. Concentration is sustaining focus and quieting the mind. Think of an artist drawing a picture of the full moon. Imagine the artist being distracted by the thought, "I can't get the radiance of the moon right," and then being able to observe that he is swept up in thinking. Aware, he can take a deep breath to recover and refocus on painting.

Observation is noticing what is occurring without reacting. Think of an astronomer peering up at the night sky through a telescope, just looking and studying. Imagine the night sky as your mind and you as the astronomer exploring what shows up in the telescope. In this open, nonjudgmental way, you gradually become aware of your thought patterns. This helps you understand yourself.

What Mindfulness Is

Mindfulness is a relationship between you as awareness and whatever you are sensing or noticing. A moment of mindfulness is when you are both aware and experiencing—in other words, you know what is going on. For example, when you mindfully press the fingertips of your right hand into the fingertips of your left hand, you are conscious of doing so.

Practice ·

Relationship - Awareness and Sensations

Press the fingertips of your right hand into the fingertips of your left hand. Notice sensations and say to yourself, "In this moment, I am aware of the sensation of pressure between my fingers." Notice the relationship between awareness and experience.

Mindfulness is being intentional. You know you are paying attention. For example, when you mindfully breathe, you pay attention to the experience of air coming in as your ribs expand and air going out as your ribs contract.

Practice ....

Intentional Attention

Notice this breath in and this breath out. Notice the movement of your ribs with your breath. You are intentionally paying attention.

Mindfulness involves choice. For example, a seated mindfulness practice begins by selecting a focal point, usually breath or a sacred word. Then, you sit comfortably and softly focus on what you have selected. When your attention wanders off, which it will do, gently bring it back and focus again. Your mind will quiet as you concentrate.

Practice ....

Choosing a Focal Point

Take a few minutes. Choose a mantra, a word that for you represents the sacred. If no word comes to mind, practice with the word *peace*. Sit comfortably and center your attention in your body. Silently and slowly, recite your chosen word or the word *peace*. When silence settles in, enjoy. When thoughts overtake you and you become aware of what is happening, choose to refocus on "peace, peace, peace."

Mindfulness connects you to the present moment, to the here and now. In breath awareness concentration practice, you focus on breath as it rises and falls moment by moment. In observing practice, you watch thoughts cross your mind moment by moment. When you observe, your mind is quiet and you are more aware of the present moment.

Practice ....

Present Moment Awareness

Pause to sit quietly. Be aware of breathing. Enjoy the moment-to-moment experience of breathing in and out.

Mindfulness is nonjudgmental. Thoughts recall the past, plan and anticipate the future, ponder your life, assess, and compare. Thoughts make internal noise and stir things up. Observing and focusing are not thoughts. They are quiet, silent, and nonreactive. When you sit in meditation, you simply observe thoughts without judgment.

Practice ....

What Mindfulness Is Not

Bring to mind a mildly judgmental thought. Be gentle—select a thought that causes very little distress, perhaps something like, "My hair does not look the best today." Say the thought out loud, then quietly state, "I am observing this critical thought."

Mindfulness is not being lost in the content of thoughts. Wandering thoughts arise when you are not focused. As stated previously, these include thoughts about the future and the past, preoccupations with yourself, and judgments/comparisons. Drift away in these thoughts and you are taken on a manufactured in-your-mind experience that disconnects you from the present moment. An example is worrying that you are too busy to get everything done.

Practice ....

Recurring Thoughts

Inquiry

Name a few recurring thoughts that take you on a ride away from the present moment.

_____

_____

_____

Mindfulness is not a state of altered consciousness. Partial and/or distorted awareness is a state of inattentiveness. Examples of this are intoxication from too much alcohol or drugs, sluggishness from excessive carbohydrates, being zoned out from watching television, and mental vacancy from Internet surfing. This state diminishes your ability to pay attention on purpose and/or be aware of what is arising in the present moment.

Practice ....

Altering Consciousness

Inquiry

In what ways do you frequently alter your consciousness?

_____

_____

_____

Mindfulness is not sleepiness. Feeling drowsy when winding down in the evening prepares you for sleep, but it is not the state of alertness associated with mindfulness. Following are examples. When you are groggy, it is dangerous to drive, as it is hard to focus on the road and detect traffic signs. When you are tired, it is next to impossible to do complicated computer work, and when you struggle to keep your eyes open, it is challenging to learn technical information.

Practice ·

Lack of Alertness

Inquiry

When do you push yourself unnecessarily or squander time on electronics when you would be better off relaxing or sleeping?

_____

_____

_____

Mindfulness is not distraction. Distraction is when your attention is divided, like when you do one thing and think about something else or when you attempt to do two things simultaneously. You notice fewer details and are less aware of here and now. Obvious examples are driving while texting, eating while inputting accounting data, listening while reading, performing job tasks while worrying about home life, and preparing food while tending to a toddler.

Practice ·

Divided Attention

Inquiry

When and how do you distract yourself?

_____

_____

_____

Mindfulness is not dissociation. Dissociation is when you are unaware of certain aspects of what you are currently experiencing or previously experienced. By definition, it is the opposite of being aware of what is occurring. This kind of disconnect is an adaptive response to traumatic events that overwhelm your coping mechanisms. It protects you from images, emotions, and sensations that are more than you can handle and is often associated with experiences that anyone would find very difficult to deal with. Examples of dissociation include forgetting aspects of painful experiences, not being able to experience grief after loss, feeling emotionally flat when recalling difficult times, experiencing emotional numbness in general, memory lapses or sketchy memory about long periods of time, not feeling life energy in your limbs, and feeling like you are outside looking in on experiences.

Practice ··

Protective Unawareness

Inquiry

When and how do you dissociate?

_____

_____

_____

Infusing Kindness into Mindfulness Practice

Mindfulness has the quality of seeing clearly. Imagine an impartial eye watching what goes on inside of and around you to help you to see things as they are. Unfortunately, this neutrality is easily distorted, thanks to the mind's preoccupation with the negative. It takes less than a moment for a dismissive, cynical afterthought to cloud clear perception. Consequently, it is wise to infuse awareness with a little kindness.

Here is an example. If you are perfectionistic, you have an inner voice that pushes you to do better. As a perfectionist, when you practice mindful breathing and attention inevitably drifts off to thoughts, the inner critic may respond with something like, "Good grief, pay attention!" You may sit up and try harder. However, harshness does not encourage mindfulness. Harshness leads to bodily tension and thoughts of being wrong. Kindness enhances mindfulness. After an automatic response of, "Good grief, pay attention," add a couple of steps. Slightly lift your hand to gesture, "Stop." Take a breath and softly whisper a soothing word, such as "gentle." Return to mindful breathing.

Practice ···

Infusing Kindness

Bring to mind a familiar thought in your head that pushes and scolds you. Write it down so you can clearly see it. Remember, this is a thought, not who you are.

_____

_____

_____

_____

Slightly raise your hand to gesture, "Stop." Take a breath. Bring to mind a gentle word or two that you might use when soothing a beloved family member or pet. Suggestions include, "Relax" "Trust," or "It is okay." Write it down to help you remember it.

_____

_____

_____

_____

Awareness of Body

Mindfulness training for stress reduction often begins with mindfulness of the body, or focusing on bodily sensations. This is a reliable way to detach attention from thoughts. You literally bring your attention back to the present by focusing on something consistently available, which is your body. This includes the sensations of breathing.

Killingsworth, a Harvard researcher, discovered that people spend nearly 50 percent of their waking hours being lost in thought (Killingsworth & Gilbert 2009). This means that their attention is wandering off in default mode network thinking, also called monkey mind or daydreaming. These authors also found that most people reported being happier when they were paying attention to what they were doing, such as walking or eating, rather than when their attention was drifting along the thought highway. This makes sense, considering both your brain's bias toward negativity and your decreased ability to notice pleasant sensations, sights, and sounds when preoccupied with thoughts.

Practice ·

Focusing on Bodily Sensations

Pause and feel both feet on the floor. If you want more sensation, firmly press your feet down. Keep your attention there for a moment. Notice that thoughts decrease.

Awareness of Thoughts

You are much more than the thoughts that cross or get stuck in your mind. You are influenced by thoughts, and they are powerful. However, you cannot be reduced to the content of your thoughts. You are also the awareness that observes thoughts.

Mindfulness shows you how to dis-identify from thoughts by putting space between yourself and your thoughts. It uses the analogy of your mind as the sky and thoughts as clouds passing by. This helps you in two ways. One is to encourage you to observe thoughts in the same way you watch clouds overhead. The other is to give you a sense of distance between you and thoughts.

Observing makes way for choice, so like a pilot flying a plane through the sky, you can navigate your way. You stay on course when you steer toward life-enhancing thoughts and fly away from pain-producing thoughts. You can move toward thoughts that encourage, comfort, and humor. It is all a matter of the training that is topic of Chapter 4.

Most thoughts fall into four categories: the past, the future, the story of you and your life, and judgment and comparison. Wisdom, also known as inner knowing, guidance, insight, and intuition, may express itself in the form of quiet thoughts. Inner guidance usually comes through when your mind is calm.

Practice ·

Observing and Categorizing Thoughts

Sit comfortably. Center in your body. Practice breath awareness for 5 or more minutes. Set a timer so you can relax, knowing that you will be notified when your predetermined time is completed. When thoughts arise, as they will, simply notice, then kindly redirect your attention to your breath. After completing this practice, recall a few of your thoughts that passed by. Write the word *past, future, story of me,* or *judgment,* along with a word or two describing specific content, in the clouds below to represent recurring thoughts.

Awareness of the World Around You

You take in information from the outside world through the five senses. Taste, touch, smell, hearing, and seeing connect you to life around you. If your inner world is too upsetting, focusing on the outer world can offer reprieve.

You only have access to sensory input in the present. You are reading these words. Later you may, through memory, recall these ideas, but right now you see letters and spaces. While looking, you are connected to the immediacy of now and liberated from the thoughts of the future and past.

The senses work together. Smell bread burning in the toaster, and you turn to look at it. Hear the doorbell ring, and you walk to the front door to look out. Taste delicious soup, and you look closely to see what is in it. This sensory coordination does not require much thought.

Sensory experience often gives rise to pleasure. Following is a list of purely delightful experiences—that is, when you mindfully pay attention to them: watching the sunrise, smelling plum blossoms, tasting homemade bread, petting a cat, listening to joyful music, smelling fresh-brewed coffee, seeing the first daffodil of spring, holding a sleepy baby.

In this next practice, you explore sensory input to familiarize yourself with intentionally doing so. Focusing on the outside when you are distressed on the inside can help you regulate your emotions and is discussed in Chapter 3. Focusing on sensory pleasure is also a way to come into present moment awareness, as discussed in Chapter 8.

Practice ....

Exploring Sensory Input

Let your attention drift back to the memory of your last meal. Recall what you ate. Now focus your attention on the room. Name three objects you see, such as curtains at the window, a lamp on a desk, a framed picture on the wall. Steadily gaze at one of these objects for a few moments. Notice that your mind quiets and you are oriented to the room and less aware of thinking.

Now focus on listening. Pause, what do you hear? Name three sounds, such as the sound of the dog breathing, your spouse's fingers clicking on the keyboard, the whirr of the air conditioner. If the room is quiet, hear silence as well. Notice that your mind quiets and becomes alert.

If you like, investigate the other senses. Continue with smelling. Notice the scent of your clothing, the smell of your hand, and an odor in the room. Explore taste. Notice the taste in your mouth; sip a beverage and notice its flavor. Finally, examine touch. Rub your thumb over your fingertips, feel the clothing against your skin, pick up an object and notice how it feels.

What was the difference between focusing on sight versus sound or other sensory experiences? Did you prefer one over another? Journal your response in the space provided.

_____

_____

_____

Awareness and Meditation

This section moves from the concrete world of body, senses, and thoughts to the intangible world of awareness. First, some context is needed. As you recall, mindfulness is the relationship between you as awareness and the object, including thoughts, that you are noticing, whether inside or outside of your body. Unlike your ever-changing body, transient experiences, and fleeting thoughts, awareness remains in you throughout your life. You *have* and *are* awareness.

A synonym for *awareness* is *consciousness*. Thus, it is not a stretch to say that you are a being of consciousness. Just consider the difference between you and a deceased body. You are alive, sentient, and aware.

Awareness is the essence of mindfulness. An effective way for you to experience awareness is to practice sitting meditation, because the aim of meditation is to be more conscious. Each time you pull back from thoughts, you recognize that you are more than what you think. You are also the aware, still observer.

It would be remiss to not introduce meditation early in this workbook. Meditation is the foundation of mindfulness practices. A meta-analysis of meditation research by Goyal and associates (2014) verifies that meditation is effective in reducing anxiety and depression. Practicing is your choice, and you can go through the workbook practices without taking time for a daily meditation. However, I wholeheartedly encourage you to be curious about and experiment with it.

You can practice meditation in numerous ways. Shortly, you have opportunity to try three forms to help you discover a type that appeals to you. First, begin with a mini-practice of the skill of simply observing.

Practice ···

Simply Observing

Sit comfortably upright in a quiet location. Begin by centering. Notice your body. Focus on breathing, or if you prefer, press your thumbs gently on your index fingers and focus on those sensations. Keep your eyes open and soft, without glancing around, and notice what you see in the area around you. Sit quietly, like a hawk perched on a high cliff watching for signs of movement. Just watching, simply being. Enjoy observing. Enjoy being aware.

Now, close your eyes or gaze down. This time you are like a hawk perched on a cliff inside your vast mind, simply watching thoughts, like clouds, pass by. Remain like the hawk, just noting, not reacting as you observe the skyscape of your mind. If critical thoughts arise, kindly refocus on breathing.

Journal about your experience with observing.

_____

_____

_____

Finding Your Meditation Practice

Take several minutes daily to practice for your wellbeing and peace. You will learn to observe, concentrate, sit quietly, and enjoy yourself. Success comes from doing the practice. Each time you sit for meditation most likely will not be a serene experience of having an empty mind, at least when you first learn the practice. It doesn't matter if your mind is busy and you spend most of your meditative session withdrawing attention from thoughts and refocusing on breath or your sacred word—you are learning and taking time for yourself. Following is a partial list of benefits accrued from meditating:

- Becoming conscious of how your mind operates
- Practicing retreating from thinking
- Learning to focus on breath or sensations on fingertips or sacred word
- Experiencing the peace of awareness
- Training your brain to serve you better

If you find that meditation seems fitting for you, incorporate it into your day by scheduling a time when you can reliably meditate. This helps to establish the habit. Over time, increase the length of your practice up to 15 or 20 minutes or more. Set a timer so you can relax and not distract yourself by looking at the time.

Below are abbreviated descriptions of three forms of meditation practice. Explore them to discover the one that most appeals to you. "Try them on" by doing them for brief amounts of time. Before beginning your meditation session, find a quiet space where you will not be interrupted or distracted.

Vipassana Meditation

Vipassana meditation, a Buddhist practice, is also called *insight meditation.* The intention is to clearly see things as they are, including the workings of your mind and the true nature of life. Following are simplified instructions. Sit comfortably upright in a quiet location. Center your attention in your body by becoming aware of your feet on the floor and hips in the chair or on the cushion. Gently close your eyes or softly gaze downward. Turn your attention to your breath. Enjoy following breath come in and go out. When thoughts arise, notice them, kindly let them be, and redirect your attention to breathing.

Sooner or later you will discover that your attention is distracted by thoughts. In response, silently whisper, "Meditating," or simply acknowledge, "Thoughts." Nod subtly and return focus to your breathing to stabilize attention. No need to tune into breathing when your mind quiets. Simply enjoy silence. When thoughts arise, refocus on breathing. When thoughts subside, enjoy inner peace. The inner experience is one of gentle focus on breath, kindly releasing thoughts and abiding in stillness. Repeat.

Practice ·

Experiencing Vipassana Meditation

Sit for 5 or more minutes of vipassana meditation.

Yoga Meditation

Yoga meditation is often taught as a spiritual form of meditation. The intention is to recognize that you are a being of higher consciousness. Following are simplified instructions. Sit comfortably upright in a quiet location. Center your attention in your body by becoming aware of your feet on the floor and hips in the chair or on the cushion. Gently close your eyes or softly gaze downward. Lightly press your thumbs on your index fingers and notice the slight sensations of energy pulsing between them. This quiets your mind and attunes awareness towards subtlety.

Then select one of two options. In the first option, imagine a golden light, like the rising sun, in the area between your eyebrows. Keep your attention focused on the white light in your forehead. As a second option, select a simple mantra that for you represents divinity, the name of a spiritual being (such as Christ or spirit) or a quality of higher consciousness (such as peace or love), or a sacred sound (such as *amen* or *om*). Then gently concentrate on either white light filling forehead or your selected mantra. The intent is to focus on higher consciousness to purify your mind. When thoughts arise, gently refocus on what you have selected. Repeat.

Practice ·

Experiencing Yogic Meditation

Experience 5 or more minutes of yogic meditation. First explore the focus on white light. Then explore focusing on a mantra.

Prayer

Centering Prayer is a spiritual form of meditation in the Christian tradition. The intention during this silent prayer is consenting to the presence and action of God. It is a method of cultivating intimacy with God—to being held tenderly, to being shown your life through the eyes of divine wisdom. Following are simplified instructions. Sit comfortably upright in a quiet location. Center your attention in your body by becoming aware of your feet on the floor and hips in the chair or on the cushion. Gently close your eyes or softly gaze downward. Select a word that for you symbolizes God, such as *Beloved* or *Abba*. Begin by silently whispering your sacred word as consent for the presence and action of God in you. When thoughts recede and all is still within, release your sacred word and abide in silence. When thoughts arise, quietly recite your word until all becomes silent and unmoving again. Repeat. When finished, sit quietly for another minute.

Practice ···

Experiencing Centering Prayer

Experience 5 or more minutes of Centering Prayer.

Write about your experience with the three forms of meditation. Decide which form is most pleasing for you and explain why.

_____

_____

_____

_____

Making Friends with Silence

Make friends with silence, and you become more contented. You have probably experienced times of ease with silence, perhaps when walking in the profound stillness of the wilderness or when resting quietly in bed on a weekend morning. Once you realize outer silence is truly safe and friendly, becoming immersed in it feels luxurious. Stillness on the inside often arises when the outer world is still. In these moments, all seems well in your world. You feel joined with something greater. Indeed, wisdom texts advocate taking time for silence and teach that in stillness you become aware of and feel connected with higher consciousness.

Silence invites inner guidance. You have probably attempted to make a simple decision at night when you were overly stressed and your mind was filled with frantic thoughts. You finally went to bed and the next morning, when your mind was quieter, the answer was obvious. When you are highly anxious, decision-making becomes impaired. Your threat system is amped up, and your mind so crowded with racing thoughts that there is little room for wisdom.

Silence replenishes your brain's attentional center, the prefrontal lobes, and according to Kirste and colleagues (2015), may regenerate brain cells. It also allows you to reflect on your inner mental and emotional states. This process of looking back at yourself, quietly and kindly, to gain perspective and understanding is nearly impossible without a little silence and space.

Silence may not yet soothe you. You may feel more comfortable keeping busy and being highly stimulated to help to keep unwanted thoughts, images, and emotions at bay. That is okay. Begin where you are at and accept your needs. If you want, approach silence gradually by adding soft music, gentle movement, or activity. After some experience, your nervous system will relax and silence will be more appealing.

Practice ··

Enjoying Silence

Spend 5 minutes in silence. Set a timer. Follow your breath if you like. Add simple movement if you prefer by doing the following. Breathe in and place hands at heart, and breathe out and place hands on lap. Alternatively, gaze at a lit candle or a flower. Experiment and find a way to enjoy 5 minutes of silence. Journal about your experience.

_____

_____

_____

_____

_____

_____

_____

_____

_____

CHAPTER 3

Emotionally Stabilize to Reduce Overwhelm, Dissociation, and Shame

---

Benefits & Clinician Notes

✓ Engagement with the parasympathetic nervous system when anxiety is rising

✓ Ability to respond with big doses of comfort/reality orientation after an unworthiness attack (further discussed in Chapter 7)

✓ Ability to soothe irritability

✓ Reorientation to here and now when numbness/dissociation take root

✓ Ability to take action to interrupt the immobilization/submission response following harassment by the inner critic (further discussed in Chapter 4)

Everyone needs a way to avoid sliding down the slippery slope into painful emotional pools. There simply is no benefit to bathing or wallowing in stagnant waters of old distress or trauma. The following techniques and practices show your patients how to interrupt the downward slide into and how to climb out of murky waters. It is not wise to avoid emotional life, but it is not beneficial to nearly drown in it. Learning to sit on the shore where this water can be examined, touched, and felt leads to understanding without reliving painful history.

Your client needs to be able to engage reasoning, at least partially, while experiencing emotions during therapy sessions. Equally important, your patients need to be aware of being in the present moment, which is what emotional stabilization techniques allow them to do. Healing requires learning to be here and now, even when looking back on there and then.

This is not a choice of either thinking or feeling. This is about de-escalating runaway emotions, preventing retraumatization and returning blood flow to the thinking brain. Without some capacity to observe and reflect, functions of prefrontal cortex, emotions cascade into reactions based on the threat system. Unintentionally, the person once again relives trauma and/or walks down painful pathways of emotional anguish, unexamined beliefs, and compensatory behaviors. Nothing is learned or healed; nothing changes in the brain.

Teaching stabilization skills is central to therapy. It is deeply compassionate because it helps your patients navigate through painful times. Here is a compelling example involving Steven (not his real name), whose daughter committed suicide. A few weeks after he returned to work, intrusive images of her death scene began interfering with his ability to focus. We talked about emotional stabilization, and I showed him a few techniques. Steven preferred doing a brief body scan (taught in this chapter), followed by gently pressing his feet down and keeping part of his attention there. He discovered that he could still listen, talk, pay attention, and process information while being aware of the sensations of his feet on the floor. In other words, he was functional. During the next session, Steven commented with a sigh of relief that he could do this anywhere, anytime, as needed, without anyone else knowing that he was regulating his emotions.

Emotional stabilization is the first responder of self-compassion, as it prevents repeated slides down the slippery slope. Restoring calm and orienting to here and now are necessary throughout the course of therapy to help your patient feel safe. In fact, cognitive therapy should not proceed until the person is sitting on solid ground where reason can be activated. This does not imply that feelings are to be squashed; it means that your patient learns to recognize what is happening and to respond wisely and with compassion.

Painful Emotional/Physiological States

Following are brief summaries of fear, dissociation, and shame, which are painful states that can persist over a long period. If you experience one or more of them, know that you are not doomed to long-term, unintentionally perpetuated emotions. You can learn and practice body-oriented mindfulness skills that soothe and orient to here and now.

Fear is your nervous system's response to threat of harm, whether the threat is of impending or imagined danger. The fear response prepares your body to fight, flight, or freeze/feign dead. Heart rate increases, muscles prepare for action, state of alertness increases, and perception of threat heightens. Anxiety results when you pair up this unconscious bodily response with thoughts of not being safe now or in an imagined future. This coupling of thoughts and physical responses occurs very rapidly, mostly outside of your awareness.

If there is actual danger, your fight or flight actions expend the revved-up energy. You run to escape or fight to protect. Then, your body can relax as your nerves calm. The freeze/feign dead response does not utilize the amped-up energy. Consequently, after the threat has passed, your nervous system may remain as alert as a doe that freezes in her tracks to avoid being detected.

Also, when threat is imagined, not imminent, or not likely, your body can remain in a state of nervous system arousal. This makes sense, as there is no immediate impetus to run or fight. Simply stated, the fear response persists when the energy is not used up. When this occurs, your nervous system needs to be reset by turning on the parasympathetic relaxation response. Fortunately, practices such as yoga and meditation are helpful in balancing the nervous system and calming the body.

Numbness/dissociation is a protection against overwhelming emotions. It is an adaptive response to early life trauma or perceived threat of great harm. It is a form of disrupted consciousness and a lack of awareness of emotions or physical sensations. This response is protective. When there are no other options, numbing out is a merciful nervous system response. However, it can persist long after danger subsides, through no fault of the individual.

This can be tricky to recognize on your own. However, a little information can help you to detect it. Not being able to feel touch or pressure on your body, feeling emotionally numb, and experiencing a sense of unreality may be indicators of dissociation. When you recognize these signs, it is time to reorient to the present by focusing on what you see and hear and pressing your feet firmly into the floor to increase physical sensations that feel safe and real.

Shame is physiological agony. It results from a severe attack and/or repeated assaults on your basic human decency. Your nervous system responds to such attacks as though you are threatened with great physical harm. The flush and startle that you may feel are first and foremost your body's fear response. Then, if these responses cascade into a sweaty, flushing, trembly state of semi-paralysis, compliance, and the wish to be invisible, you experience shame. It is important to recognize that shame is about fear, immobilization, and submission, which sounds like the freeze/feign dead response. Alternatively, your nervous system may kick into fight mode and you angrily, verbally ward off your attacker.

You can interrupt shame. Doing so begins by learning emotional stabilization skills. The downward spiral needs to be stopped. (See Chapter 7 for healing protocol for shame.)

Emotional Stabilization Skills

Painful emotions are experiences of a distressed nervous system coupled with the thoughts generated by your mind. They are truly a mind/body occurrence. Understand that emotions show up in your physiology, and it makes sense that alleviating emotional disturbance involves calming your nervous system. You soothe your body to ease your mind.

In the sections that follow are descriptions of body-based emotional stabilization skills. Find one that works well for you.

The following brief body scan is designed for emotional stabilization. Its benefits are listed below.

- Distraction from escalating, painful emotions by the redirection of attention to sensations of muscles and flesh
- Interruption of dissociation and the bringing of attention to bodily sensations that feel safe, substantial and real
- Increase of awareness of the present moment through concentration on current bodily sensations
- Ease of ability to remember and do this practice

Practice ··

Brief Body Scan for Emotional Stabilization

Focus on and feel both feet on the floor. Focus on and feel your hips in the chair. Focus on and feel your spine rising up. Now, choose which feels better, concentrating on either your feet or your hips. Keep your attention directed toward your feet or hips.

Journal your response to body scan focus. Do you have a preference of focusing on feet on floor or hips in chair?

_____

_____

_____

_____

Tip for dissociation or intrusive memories/images that help create emotions: Press feet firmly on floor to increase sensation. Pressing feet down creates a strong sensation that is attention grabbing and thus beneficial when you feel numb or experience high internal distress.

Mindful Looking and Listening—Sensory Input

Using your eyes and ears to orient you to the space around you is a form of concentration mindfulness. Looking around and listening to sounds can emotionally stabilize you when the outer world is orderly and your emotions escalate. Its benefits are listed below.

- Redirection of attention away from distress
- Anchoring to attention in safe surroundings

- Orientation to outer world when dysregulated on inside
- Reality testing to current location
- Protection against pain-producing ruminations and anticipations
- Ease of ability to remember and do this practice

Practice ···

Orienting to the Outer World
By Looking and Listening

Open your eyes. Look around you. Name three things that you see. Select one thing at which to softly gaze and keep your attention there. A soft gaze is not the darting gaze or wide-eyed stare of fear.

Alternatively, keep eyes open so that you know where you are, and focus intently on subtle sounds. Name two or three sounds. Select one and keep attention there.

Journal your response to sensory focus. Do you have a preference of either seeing or listening?

_____

_____

_____

_____

Mindful Breathing Practices

Mindful breathing is a concentration practice. While it is an effective emotional regulator for many, it is not for all. For some it calms and distracts attention away from distress. For others, breath focus brings attention to chest area discomfort or dysregulated breathing. If it does not comfort you, discontinue it and utilize another form of emotional regulation. Its benefits are listed below.

- Slowing of the breath and engagement of the relaxation response. Breathing is a function of both the autonomic and voluntary nervous systems. Therefore, when you intentionally lengthen the exhalation and deepen the inhalation, the parasympathetic nervous system turns on
- Lowering of anxiety
- Quieting of the thinking mind by redirecting attention toward breathing
- Anchoring of attention to the present moment

Following are four breathing practices. Try them on to find one that most appeals to you.

Practice ....

Even Breathing

Breathe in for the count of five, breathe out for the count of five. Repeat the cycle five times. Stay in your comfort zone. Alternatively, bring hands together and touch fingertips. Gently press your thumbs together for the first count of the in breath, index fingers together to signify the second, and continue, finally pressing little fingers together for the fifth breath. Reverse the movement during counting for the exhalation, beginning with little fingers and ending with thumbs. Repeat the cycle five times.

Practice ....

Breath Retention Practice

Breathe in for the count of four, hold your breath for the count of four, exhale for the count of eight. Go at a pace comfortable for you. Count more quickly for the first couple of rounds to make it easier, then gradually count more slowly. Repeat the cycle five times.

Practice ....

Follow the Complete Breath

Notice breath as it comes in and as it goes out. Repeat a couple of times. Now, follow the complete breath in and the complete breath out, from beginning to end. Gently keep your attention on the entire breathing cycle. Repeat five times.

Practice ....

Breathing with Hand Movements

Relax your hands on your lap, palms facing up. Breathe in and gently lift your hands a few inches up in the air, breathe out, turn palms down, and gently rest hands on lap. Find a simple rhythm that is relaxing for you. Repeat five times.

Journal about your experience with the breathing practices. Note which practice, if there was one, that seemed most pleasing for you.

_____

_____

_____

Mindful Yoga

Simple, mindful yoga movement can be an effective form of emotional stabilization. This concentration practice combines breath awareness and simple movement. Like the other practices, this may appeal to some more than others. Yoga movements create more bodily sensations than breathing practices. Increasingly, treatment centers for trauma recommend yoga. Because trauma often involves shame, mindful yoga that involves self-awareness and movement away from self-judgment can be a good way to reduce shame and increase self-acceptance. The benefits of a simple yoga practice are listed below.

- Care and respect for your body
- Activation of the parasympathetic nervous system, which lowers anxiety
- Increase in ability to tolerate and enjoy bodily sensations, which decreases dissociation
- Quieting of the thinking mind, including the voice of the inner critic
- Creation of a pleasant experience in the present moment
- Distraction from distress

There are many forms of yoga. If you find the following practice pleasing, you may want to search for a trauma-informed yoga class, a beginning yoga class, a gentle yoga class, or a restorative yoga class.

Practice ....

Simple Yoga Practice

Following are easy poses that may feel pleasant and be beneficial. Have a couple of pillows nearby. Dress in comfortable clothing.

1. Lie on floor with arms at side, knees in air, feet on floor under your knees and hip width apart.

2. Lift hips several inches up in the air. Gently roll hips back down to floor. Repeat five or more times.

3. Hug knees to chest. Gently roll body side to side.

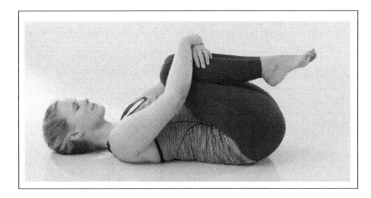

4. Roll onto right side and come to comfortable seated pose.

5. Inhale, lift arms up, exhale, place right hand on floor beside right hip, and reach left arm up and over the body so that you feel a stretch in the left side of your torso. Stay here for five breaths. Inhale, bring both arms overhead, exhale, place left hand on floor beside left hip and reach right arm up and over the body so that you feel a stretch in the right side of your body. Remain here for five breaths.

6. Inhale, sit upright, bring both arms overhead. Exhale, place your hands over your heart. Remain here for five breaths.

7. Inhale, lift arms up, exhale, place right hand on floor beside right hip and left hand on right knee in spinal rotation. Take five comfortable breaths. Inhale, lift arms up and face center, exhale, place left hand on floor beside left hip and right hand on left knee in a spinal rotation. Take five comfortable breaths.

8. Inhale, lift arms up and face center, exhale, bring your hands to your heart. Sitting here, recite the following self-care mantra: "My dear, I am here, I am learning to take care of you." Repeat a couple more times. Bow forward.

9.   Lie on the floor with a pillow under your head and also one under your knees if you have lower back discomfort and rest quietly for 5 or more minutes. If this is uncomfortable, you may rest on your right side or face down. You choose. If possible, enjoy silence, or if preferred, listen to meditative music.

In the space below, write about how you feel after completing this simple practice.

_____

_____

_____

Mindful Walking

Mindful walking is a pleasant practice of walking and being aware that you are walking, step by step. It is walking for the sake of walking rather than walking to arrive at some future destination. You walk and focus on the sensations of your feet stepping as a way of keeping your attention in your body. A moving meditation, you generally walk a little slower than your usual pace, so that you don't slip into your familiar walking habit.

The benefits of mindful walking are listed below.

• Lowering of the nervous system's stress response, thus reducing anxiety and irritability
• Creation of physical sensation, which takes focus off default network thoughts
• Distraction of attention away from upsetting emotions and unhelpful thoughts
• Stimulation of sensory awareness of sights and sounds when walking outdoors
• Creation of a pleasant experience in the present moment

Practice ·

Mindful Walking

Select a pleasant place to walk, perhaps outdoors, weather permitting. Choose an accessible route, such as around the back yard or up and down the block. Indoors, you can simply walk through rooms. Start by standing and gently pressing both feet down. Lift one leg, feeling the weight of your body on the other leg. Switch sides and lift the other leg. Again, feel each foot pressing down, then begin walking. Pay attention to and feel your feet touching the floor or the earth, heel to toe and heel to toe. Walk in a comfortable cadence so that walking is enjoyable. You are walking and paying attention to walking—that is all. When your mind wanders, simply refocus on walking.

Journal your response to mindful walking.

_____

_____

_____

_____

This section taught you options for stabilizing your emotions when they are moving into overwhelm and escalation. Which form(s) appeal to you? Practice your preferred form(s) daily for a few minutes to cultivate it as a resource that you will remember to do when you are distressed.

In the journaling space below, jot down your preference(s) and a time of day when you could briefly practice your emotional stabilization skills.

_____

_____

_____

_____

CHAPTER 4

Practices to Observe and Choose Thoughts

Benefits & Clinician Notes

✓ Experience of the impact of thoughts to understand their power

✓ Study, categorization, and naming of thoughts to increase capacity to observe them

✓ Exploration of the story of identity

✓ Ability to relate kindly to inner critic and to thoughts associated with physical pain

✓ Choice of helpful thoughts

This chapter delivers the essential teaching that you are more than the thoughts that pass through your mind. A Buddhist nun Pema Chodron (2001) teaches the analogy of your mind being like the sky and your thoughts being like the weather. This creates a helpful image of your mind as a vast space and passing thoughts as clouds that create all kinds of weather.

There is no denying that thoughts can powerfully affect you. They generate strong physiological responses and join together into perspectives and attitudes that are resistant to change. Thanks to the negativity bias of the brain, thoughts that scare, discourage, and criticize are highly stimulating. Without training, your patients become ensnared by those kinds of thoughts. Then they are pulled along in jet streams of thoughts. To stay with the weather metaphor, being swept up in thoughts can feel as miserable as being caught in a thunderstorm without rain gear.

You may have to repeatedly teach your patients that they are more than their thoughts. It is a challenging yet important idea to grasp. Teach your patients that they can disengage from thoughts and take refuge from thought storms. Show them how to relate to thoughts rather than get lost in them so they can protect themselves from the lightning bolt of shame, the hurricane of panic, and the tornado of negative thoughts. It does require some education and training, but the benefits are tremendous.

Here is an example from my practice about relating to the voice of the inner critic (taught in this chapter). The day I educated lovely Michele (not her real name) about the voice of the inner critic, including how to kindly interrupt it, was a day of liberation for her. First I taught her how to recognize and give the inner critic a name. Michele named hers after her grandfather. Then, we discussed how the words of her inner critic perpetuated racism, sexism, and verbal abuse inside herself and reinforced low self-worth.

After this discussion, I taught her to gently raise her hand to interrupt the inner critic and also to put space between herself and its message. We practiced several times then sat quietly. The next session, Michele tearfully reported that she felt love for herself for the first time and that she had been raising her hand a lot. She realized that she was not the old story of unworthiness that the inner critic had kept alive. In the following months, Michele made significant lifestyle changes that reflected her growing self-love. Naturally, at times she slid back and believed the old story. But with therapeutic reinforcement, she was able to climb back up and reclaim her inherent dignity. At our last session, we agreed that the skill of climbing up and out would be with her for as long as needed.

Teaching your patients how to relate to thoughts rather than be lost in them empowers them. The first step is learning to pull back from thoughts so they can be observed. A little distance gives perspective and the ability to say "No way I am going down that stormy highway in my mind," followed by a choice to move along a more life-affirming pathway.

Experience the Impact of Thoughts

Your mind and body are interconnected. What you think impacts your posture and your muscular strength and even alters your body's chemistry. It is helpful to understand this conceptually and liberating to get this experientially. Once you feel the effect that the content of thoughts has on your body, you become more motivated to practice observing your thoughts. Understand the power of thoughts, and you become motivated to disengage from harmful ones and concentrate on helpful ones.

This simple exercise demonstrates how much thoughts influence your physiology. All thoughts, whether of the past, future, judgment, the story of you and your life, or even wisdom create bodily experiences in the present moment. You can discover this for yourself by going down memory lane. You can pull up thoughts from the past, and they will affect you now.

Practice ....

Experiencing How Thoughts Influence Physiology

Bring up a memory of a happy surprise. Close your eyes and linger there. Notice what happens in your body. Write down a few words describing your experience.

_____

_____

_____

Bring up a memory of something funny. Close your eyes and linger there. Notice what happens in your body. Write down a few words describing your experience.

_____

_____

_____

Bring up a memory of a disappointment. Close your eyes and linger there. Notice what happens in your body. Write down a few words describing your experience.

_____

_____

_____

Bring up a memory of an irritation. Close your eyes and linger there. Notice what happens in your body. Write down a few words describing your experience.

_____

_____

_____

Bring up a memory of someone being kind to you. Close your eyes and linger there. Notice what happens in your body. Write down a few words describing your experience.

_____

_____

_____

Nonjudgmental Observing of Thoughts—Watch Thoughts Go By

You may know the peaceful feeling of resting in a lounge chair watching clouds drift by. You sit, relaxed and alert, enjoying clouds as they morph and move. You are just noticing, not reacting. You are here; clouds are there. That is all—no judgments about clouds being good or bad, right or wrong. You don't have to do anything in relationship to the clouds.

Obviously, if a storm brews, you choose to take cover, but first things first. You can't go to safety if you are unaware of approaching winds and rain, so awareness comes first. Clouds can cause turbulent weather on the outside, but arguably, thoughts can cause even more damaging weather. Obviously, the effects of thoughts are on the inside. That is where they form emotions, physical sensations, perceptions, and enduring beliefs. Many people do not know how to take refuge from thought storms. Doing so begins with nonjudgmental observing of thoughts.

Practice ·

Nonjudgmental Observing of Thoughts

Sit comfortably. Read these instructions and spend a minute or so on the first part followed by a few minutes on the second part of this practice of nonjudgmental observing.

First, become aware of your body. Next, if you are near a window or outdoors, look at the sky. Otherwise, look around the room. Just observe what is in your visual field without judging what you see. Simply notice. Take in information—that is all.

Second, when ready, close your eyes. Gently focus on breathing. Using your inner eye, watch thoughts that arise. When one passes by, kindly call it a thought. Silently whisper, "Thought" and softly redirect your attention to breathing.

Journal a few words to describe your experience of nonjudgmental observing.

_____

_____

_____

Categorizing Thoughts

You, the one who experiences thoughts, are also the one who can watch them and relate to them wisely. Remember, mindfulness implies a relationship between you as awareness and what you are aware of. Even though thoughts don't seem like "things," it is helpful to conceive of them as "objects" that you observe and study, not unlike clouds in the sky. Establish some space between you as awareness and the thoughts you observe, and you experience relief.

There are additional steps that reduce the power of thoughts that depress, frighten, and reinforce low self-worth. After observing such thoughts, you can categorize them. Doing so reveals how frequently these thoughts show up and clearly establishes space between you and them, the space needed for you to make the compassionate choices taught in Chapter 6.

In Chapter 1, in discussing the "default network," I described four pathways of thoughts: past, future, story of "me and my life," and analysis/comparison, otherwise known as judgment. I used the word *pathways* to underscore how recurring thoughts create neuronal tracks in your brain. These four pathways can also be characterized as categories of thoughts. In the following practice, I refer to *past*, *future*, *"story of me,"* and *judgment* as categories.

Flavor this practice with kindness and nonjudgment. In other words, be gentle with yourself. This practice reinforces space between you and thoughts. Become familiar with categorizing thoughts, and then, throughout the day when a recurring thought that causes you emotional pain comes up, you can breathe and whisper the category it falls under. For example, the thought, "I won't have enough time to get everything done," falls under the category of *future*.

Practice ···

Categorizing Thoughts

Sit comfortably upright. Read the instructions and spend a few minutes on the first part, followed by a 5 or more minutes on the second part.

First, center in your body. Gently focus on breath coming in and going out.

Second, when ready, softly close your eyes. Be aware of breathing or focus on thumb/index finger touch and simply observe thoughts. When a thought passes by, kindly whisper the category it belongs to: *past*, *future*, *"story of me,"* or *judgment*. Then, breathe.

Which category of thoughts showed up the most during this practice? Write a few words about what you want to remember from this practice.

_____

_____

_____

_____

Writing Thoughts Down

You can magnify the benefits of the previous practice. Select the category of thoughts that was most prevalent for you. In the set of boxes on the next page, write the name of the predominant category, such as *"story of me"* in the top box. In the six boxes underneath, list specific thoughts that belong in that category. Include some that arose during the above practice and add other familiar thoughts that often cross your mind.

Following is an example for someone who suffers from unworthiness.

Story of Me

I smile on the outside and no-body knows the real me.	I know I am loved but don't feel loved.	I don't know what is wrong with me.
I want my granddaughter to be a better person than I am.	I wear pretty clothes to feel better about my self.	No one knows how insecure I am.

Place the workbook, with this page up, on the floor in front of you. Notice the space between you and the thoughts you listed. This reinforces the reality that you are more than the content of your thoughts. From this distance, you can see thoughts without reacting to them.

Seeing Thoughts as Inner Environment

It is easy to look around at the furniture in the area in which you are seated. Your eyes orient you to the surrounding space. It takes some practice, but envisioning the thoughts in your mind as external to your innermost self is a liberating step. It is obvious that there is space between you and the chairs across the room and less apparent that there is space between you and thoughts. Negative and scary thoughts feel intimately close because of how they affect your body. It feels as though you are inside of thoughts rather than the other way around. It is challenging to learn to look at them the way you do lamps and tables. Yet the effort it takes reaps huge rewards.

Imagine being able to whisper, "I recognize you" to thoughts about not being good enough. Envisioning the thoughts as "up there in your mind" allows you to whisper, "story of me." Looking at thoughts helps you to dis-identify from them and is a reminder that who you are is more than thoughts.

The metaphor of your mind as sky helps you to appreciate how vast your mind is. It is relieving to picture thoughts as rolling by overhead. However, some thoughts seem closer, as if they have taken up residence with you. These are your recurring, familiar thoughts. They are the ones that perpetuate low self-worth and unhappiness and potentially are ones that generate compassion and happiness.

Such thoughts can be viewed as occupying rooms of a mansion in your mind. In the mansion metaphor, you can imagine walking from one room to another. You can move out of rooms of pain and into rooms of wisdom, compassion, and happiness. You can fill rooms with life-affirming thoughts. Spend more time in rooms that represent desired states of mind, and you change your brain and your life.

Practice ··

Envisioning Thoughts Occupying Rooms of a Mansion

Imagine a mansion of many rooms in your mind. The image on the next page has rooms enough to list familiar thought occupants. You may want to add other rooms and other descriptions. There are probably many rooms in your interior mansion, including ones for self-care, play, creativity, courage, patience, humor, strength, perseverance, and love, even though they are not listed below. This visual is a way for you to conceptualize your thoughts as circulating around your inner self, the one who is aware, who sees. If you like, envision your inner self as a clear, brilliant diamond or as consciousness.

In this metaphor, you live in the mansion, but you are not the rooms of the mansion. Consider the possibility of being able to roam from room to room and to choose which rooms in which to spend your time. Notice that the rooms for compassion and happiness are larger than the others.

Write a word or two typifying the content of thoughts that live in each room.

A Mansion of Thoughts

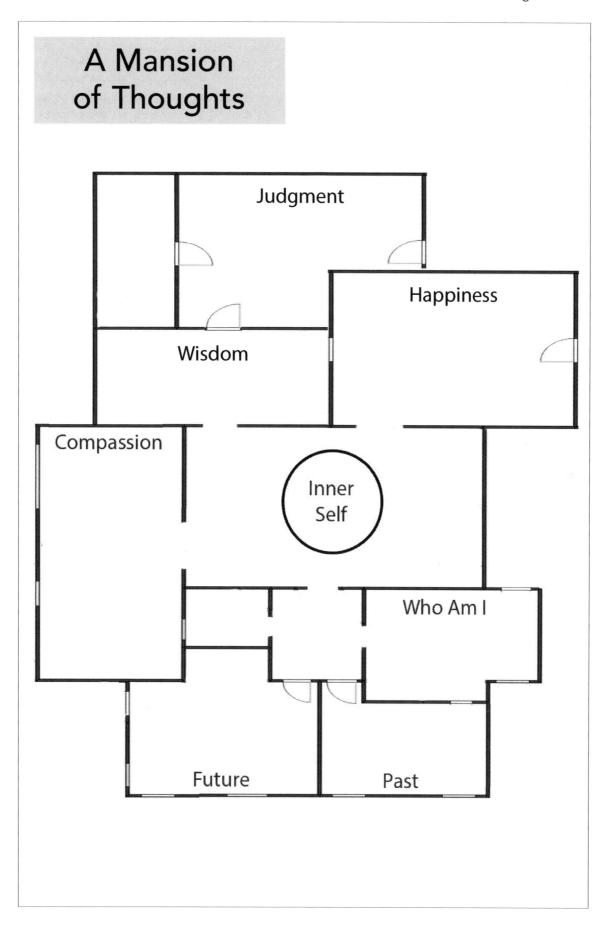

Journal about what you discovered in this practice.

_____

_____

_____

_____

_____

_____

_____

Relating to the "Story of Me"

It is just the way it is that during your developing years, you formed a sense of identity. Everybody does. You were given a name shortly after birth that you identify as your name for the rest of your life, unless you change it. Your name, as close to you as it seems, is not who you truly are! Your name is a marker of the social brain.

The process of identity making evolves over the course of childhood. Thanks to interpersonal neurobiology, you soaked in the attitudes of your community; the biases of your family; the love, care, mistreatment, and traumas that directly or indirectly affected you. By the time you reached adolescence, your story of who you are had taken form, although not very consciously.

The story of identity answers four central questions. Am I loveable? Am I competent? How does my worth compare with that of others? What is possible; what life opportunities are options for me? The answers fuse together and indicate your assessed worth as a human being. As weird as it may seem, that's what your story of identity boils down to. The good news is that who you are cannot be reduced to the content of your thoughts, including this particular story. You can relate wisely to your "story of me," just like you can do with other thoughts.

In essence, your story of identity is not who you are. Nor can it reflect your worthiness. Your preciousness shines from your inner self, otherwise called consciousness or the divinity with which you came to earth. Granted, it takes considerable practice to wrap your mind around the truth that your story is not you! Yet, every moment of practice gives relief and opens the door of clear seeing about who you are.

Practice ....

Composing the "Story of Me"

Using few words, mindfully look at your story without collapsing into your story. Briefly journal your answers to the following questions.

Am I lovable?

_____

_____

_____

_____

Am I competent?

_____

_____

_____

_____

Compared with others, am I valuable?

_____

_____

_____

_____

What is possible; what life options are available for me?

_____

_____

_____

_____

What brief phrase captures the essence of your story of who you are?

_____

_____

_____

_____

Now, push the workbook a little distance away, with this page open to create some space between you, as the aware witness, and your story of identity. Here you are, looking at a story that has had tremendous impact on your life. Now softly whisper its true name, "story of me."

Breathe deeply, feel your feet on the floor.

Relating to the Voice of the Inner Critic

Your mind engages in analytical thinking, which is fortunate since this makes maturing possible. Look at some of the hallmarks of human maturity: understanding the relationship between choice and consequence, having a moral compass, being responsible, making wise decisions, keeping commitments, living by values, experiencing humility, and being kind. These capacities rely on self-reflection.

Your remarkable capacity for analytical thinking can be used for beneficence or malice. For example, you may spend considerable time pondering your life. The question is whether this self-examination is used to help or harm. When the threat system is in overdrive, critical thinking becomes criticism turned against yourself in a running, scolding commentary. You probably know the voice that says, "You didn't get it right," "You need to do better," "You made a fool of yourself." For some, inner criticism comes in the form of "I" statements, such as "I can't get it right." Whether it speaks as "you" or "I," this voice puts you down. Following the route of neuroplasticity, the voice of the inner critic becomes entrenched after enough repetitions and seemingly takes on a life of its own.

You, like everyone, have a voice in your head that comments on others as well as yourself. These comments fall into the default mode network under the thought category of *judgment*. A few people distort toward "All is good, and all is well" in their assessments. More people distort toward "Something is wrong," and most people are notably more critical of themselves than of others. Unfortunately, if you have an identity of "not good enough," your inner critic may attack with cruel commentary. It is an unrelenting reinforcer of low self-worth.

You can learn to recognize, understand, and kindly relate to the voice of the inner critic. Doing so begins by becoming informed. Much has been written about this harsh aspect of self because it is so prevalent. Although you may feel alone with your inner critic, having one is a shared human experience, at least in Western cultures. It seems that everyone has a voice that scolds, monitors, and harangues self and others. The issue is not having an inner critic but how you relate to it.

Consider the following about the inner critic:

- The voice of the inner critic dismisses, bullies, and threatens and is generally wounding. Its origins are harsh treatment in early life; traumatic incidents that demean; societal beliefs that rank the value of people based on skin color, ethnicity, sex, sexual orientation, and age; and social institutions that discriminate according to entrenched biases.

- The inner critic does not have your best interests at heart. It reinforces and perpetuates distress in your nervous system and generally keeps you upset. Remember, the human brain is capable of violence, and violence is the food source of the inner critic. What else could energize a voice that nitpicks, nags, and spews disgust and scorn? It lets you know that you should have done better, you should be different, you can't do better, and you are foolish. Clearly this is not a voice by which you want to be guided. Its words cover your inner essence with muck.

- The inner critic is a one-song band. It only knows how to keep you down. It does not know how to support and encourage. Steady reassurance is the job of the compassionate self, which you study and cultivate in Chapter 6.

- The inner critic is a residual voice of the past that carries on into the present. The inner critic's harsh and highly stimulating voice commands your attention and creates a painful present moment. Often, it takes a strong response like clapping your hands, stretching your arms, standing up, moving your body, or doing a chore to divert your attention away.

Practice ···

Mindfully Relating to the Inner Critic

When you are ready, take the following steps.

Name your inner critic. Simply calling it "inner critic" is sufficient. Consider naming it after some person, perhaps from your earlier years, whose voice and words it parrots. Or, use a descriptive word, such as *jackhammer*.

_____

_____

_____

Add some understanding. Briefly write about the origins of your inner critic. No need to elaborate and become embroiled in painful memories—keep some distance.

_____

_____

Raise a hand up to acknowledge the inner critic. Address it by the name you gave it. Gently move your hand away to create a little space between you, as the aware witness, and the inner critic. This is not a rejection; this is a way to establish some breathing room between you and the voice of the inner critic. Quietly say "Not now."

Refocus. Feel your feet on the floor and breathe. In Chapter 6 on self-compassion, you learn to take a next step, which is responding to the inner critic with kindness. For now, clap your hands, get up, and go do something purposeful or pleasing.

You just practiced rescuing yourself from the voice of the inner critic. You used mindfulness to come out from under its spell.

Write about the experience of naming, understanding, acknowledging, and refocusing as a mindful way of relating to the voice of the inner critic.

_____

_____

_____

_____

Releasing the Second Arrow of Pain

Physical pain associated with accidents and illness is an inevitable and shared human experience. It is also difficult and exhausting to endure. And, chronic pain is downright depressing.

Your body and mind are interconnected, and thoughts about pain intensify suffering. They engage in a spiraling cycle of pain, pain commentary thoughts, and more pain. Thich Nhat Hahn (2014) refers to the original injury or sickness as the first arrow that penetrates your body. He refers to provocative comments about the pain as the second arrow. The second arrow of thoughts pierces the same place and plunges the first arrow more deeply into the flesh, thus inflaming the wound, sometimes significantly so.

The self-talk that escalates pain pertains to "if only," "what if," and "story of me" statements. "If only" refers to the past: "If only I had taken better care of my health." "If only I had listened to my wife." "If only I had taken a different route home." You can hear the agony of regret and self-blame.

"What if" refers to the future: "What if it never gets better?" "What if it gets worse?" "What if I can't work?" "What if this wipes out my retirement savings or we lose the house?" You can hear the fear.

The "story of me" reinforces the old narrative of identity: "Just my luck." "What else could I expect?" "That's the way it goes for me." You can hear how pain is woven into the story of who you are, as if pain is somehow your fault because of who you are.

Your body and mind are joined. Physical pain amps up the nervous system and so do second arrow thoughts. Pain decreases and healing increases when the body relaxes. Deep breathing, walking, gentle yoga, plenty of rest, and meditation soothe the body. Find what works for you and increase self-care when you are in pain. Your body needs you as an intimate ally to be there for it, to offer reassurance and talk kindly to it. For your body's sake, become familiar with and relate wisely to thoughts that exacerbate pain.

....

Mindfully Relating to "Second Arrow" Thoughts

Name "if only" thoughts that are familiar to you.

_____

_____

_____

_____

Name "what if" thoughts that are familiar to you.

_____

_____

_____

_____

Name "story of me" thoughts that are familiar to you.

_____

_____

_____

_____

Remember, thoughts can wound you, and you are more than thoughts. Become acquainted with thoughts that cause distress so that when one comes along, you can raise your hand and gently create space between you and it. Breathe deeply, and with your other hand touch your heart, as if to say "Compassion, be with me now."

Mindfulness and Choosing Life-Affirming Thoughts

Thoughts are indeed powerful and can cause anguish and illness when they run amok. Unhelpful thoughts rev up the threat system and the negativity bias of the brain. Ruminations and fearful anticipations solidify the story of self as insufficient and the belief about life being generally dangerous. Unchecked, these thoughts strengthen the same old neuropathways in your mind and make you increasingly miserable.

Your mind inherently reacts to significant events, including traumatic ones, as it processes images, sounds, physical sensations, conversations, and emotions. These reactions may gradually become inactive, or they can last for a long time. The more evocative the experience, the deeper the imprint in neuropathways.

Fortunately, you can help your mind out. Liken your mind to an untamed horse: When distress-causing thoughts persist, your mind is comparable to a wild stallion that terrifies you as its rider. But the feral tendency of your mind can be tamed. You can train it by doing the following. Observe and name thoughts that do not help you. Raise your hand and say "Not now." Feel your feet on the floor, take a deep breath, and regain balance. This quiets the inner stallion and begins domesticating your mind.

Mindfulness is a relationship between you as observer and the contents of your thoughts. Mindfulness makes choice possible and allows you to steer your thinking mind into calm pastures. It is possible for you to be a kind master who guides your mind. It sure beats hanging on to a runaway stallion for dear life. It takes some training, but every practice session strengthens your capacity.

Select life-affirming thoughts. Why not? It is better than the alternative of being under the influence of thoughts that wound. Choosing thoughts is a form of mind training. First, you need to know where you want to go. Most likely, you want to be in pastures of self-acceptance, compassion, contentment, and happiness, which are the green meadows of the affiliation system. This is the land where you experience life's sanctity.

In a moment, you will have the opportunity to list thoughts that feel beneficial, but first a discussion about choosing thoughts. Thoughts need to feel resonant so that you emotionally digest rather than reject them. Below, after each quality of the affiliation system, are examples of thoughts that may help in your thought selection.

Self-acceptance. If you want to accept yourself, but a thought such as, "I accept myself as I am" sounds fictional, select a thought that rings more true for you. Perhaps a thought like, "I want to learn to like myself" feels genuine.

Contentment. If you want contentment but find that a thought such as, "In this moment I am grateful for eyes that see beauty" sounds insincere, select a thought that feels more authentic. Perhaps a thought like, "I am willing to find one thing I am grateful for" is doable.

Happiness. If you want happiness but find that a thought such as, "I have something to be happy about in this moment" sounds false, select a thought feels true. Perhaps a thought like, "I remember this happy time" brings a soft smile.

Self-compassion. If you want self-compassion but find that a thought such as, "My dear, I am here for you" sounds hollow, select a thought that touches your heart. Perhaps a thought like, "May you experience healing, may you find peace" stirs your yearning for compassion. (Self-compassion practices are taught in Chapter 6.)

Practice ···

Selecting Life Affirming Thoughts

Write a couple of thoughts under each category that feel palatable for you. Be curious and experimental with this brain training.

Self-acceptance

_____

_____

_____

_____

Contentment

_____

_____

_____

_____

Happiness

_____

_____

_____

_____

Self-compassion

_____

_____

_____

_____

CHAPTER 5

Practices for Distress and Emotional Aliveness

Benefits & Clinician Notes

✓ Learning to not fear emotions

✓ Cultivating specific skill sets for taking care of emotions

✓ Strengthening emotional resiliency

✓ Having the ability to comfort self while experiencing emotions

---

This chapter is about learning how to be a loving mother to your emotions. This is tender work, because emotions expose vulnerability and vulnerability can feel threatening. Accordingly, it is often easier to first deal with thoughts, which is why this chapter is placed after the last one. Obviously, emotions and thoughts coexist, and therapy is not a step-by-step procedure. Yet, it can be helpful to study thoughts and emotions sequentially.

It becomes safer to approach emotions after you have taught your patients how to de-escalate, be aware of their bodies, and anchor to the present moment. You sure want to reduce the risks of retraumatization and emotional shutdown. With the skills of emotional stabilization on board, helping your patients approach emotions restores their emotional aliveness and human vulnerability.

Learning to take care of emotional life is often a slow process. A brief review of the defense mechanisms you studied in graduate school helps to explain why. Most defense mechanisms, learned through parent and societal modeling, are ways of dealing with emotional life in general. They include suppression, denial, avoidance, intellectualization, somatization, and regression. As coping skills, they are at times merciful, as they can prevent overwhelm. The defense mechanism of dissociation seems to be less learned and more automatic. Part of the brain's survival mode, it is protective and takes over when unbearable emotions surpass your ability to cope.

Defense mechanisms become habitual. They can take on a life of their own and persist when no longer needed. At some point, patients may catch glimpses of whatever happened or didn't happen that sourced low self-worth, anxiety, and/or depression. When this material surfaces, your patients may meet some resistance and want to avoid emotional discomfort. This is understandable, since defense mechanisms protected them from raw emotions. Yet, the time comes to learn to allow and kindly breathe through emotions. This does not imply that patients benefit from soaking in painful emotional pools. They do not, which is why you teach stabilization skills.

Difficulties with emotions also stem from societal misunderstanding about emotional life. As a culture, we are not at ease with showing emotions. A prime example is cultural discomfort with grief. Additionally, we are impacted by societal attitudes about emotions, including the familiar ones that say "Suck it up," "Don't be weak," and "Don't let it show."

Finally, there is internal thought reactivity about approaching emotions. The inner critic may spout thoughts such as "You are such a weakling" and "You are making a fool of yourself." When patients suffer from unworthiness, their narrative of who they are may cry out with thoughts such as "I just want to disappear," "This proves I am flawed," and "I cannot do this." These kinds of thoughts magnify emotional anguish. They can be recognized and treated as second arrows, as discussed in Chapter 4.

This clinical example highlights the advantage of approaching emotions with mercy. Betty (not her real name), a middle-aged woman with an autoimmune disease, chronic pain, and episodes of depression, practiced treating her body and emotions with kindness. Toward the end of therapy, Betty reported that rather than fighting depression, she diligently practiced welcoming it as a guest in her inner mansion. She added that since she stopped fighting depression, it doesn't take up as much space.

Here is a sample conversation in which Betty opens the door and offers her version of MERCY, a practice taught in this chapter, to depression. When depression knocks, Betty meets it by saying "Hello, depression, my old friend. Tell me what is going on." She listens for an answer and then responds with something like "I am sorry you are having a rough time." She massages her arms and legs to soothe her achy body. Then, she finds something simple that she can say "yes" to, like another opportunity to be kind to herself, a comfortable bed, a warm cup of tea, or sunlight shining in the window

Mindfulness of Emotions

Mindfulness is a relationship between you as observer and what is occurring. Mindfulness of emotions is the ability to experience a little space between you, as awareness, and the emotions you experience. The goal is to be aware of and realize that you are more than emotions. Without this realization, you can be subsumed by emotions and pulled down by their force.

Not having space means that you are at risk of careening down the cliff into the pool of painful emotions. It is worth re-emphasizing that there is no benefit to swimming in pools of despair, anxiety, sadness, and anger. Doing so just reinforces the neuronal pathways of that particular emotion. In fact, another lap of swimming increases the likelihood of greater intensity and longer time spent in that emotional pool. When you want to swim, seek clear, calm water.

Use your intentionality to help yourself. Breathe! Breathe, and you create space that releases a little of the emotional pull. This prevents the slide down the slippery cliff, thus de-escalating fear, sadness, or anger.

Next, name the emotion and speak it out loud. This establishes you as observer. Recognize that you are experiencing an emotion, and you are more than the emotion. These steps help restore blood flow to the thinking brain and enable you to choose to take care of yourself.

Practice ···

Experiencing Space Between You, as Awareness, and an Emotion

Bring to mind an emotion that tends to upset you. Select an easier emotion, not a highly distressing one, since you are still learning this skill. Breathe!

Name the emotion in the space below.

_____

State out loud: "There is a little space between me as observer and me as experiencer of this emotion."

Breathe!

Notice that you acknowledged this emotion and mindfully created a little space in your mind.

Taking Care of Emotions Like a Loving Parent

Toddlers are not able to emotionally self-regulate. Their lower brain center, which includes the threat, affiliation, and drive systems, is operational. Their higher brain center, particularly the prefrontal lobes, which give capacity to concentrate, intentionally observe, make wise decisions, regulate emotions, and understand cause and effect, is barely on line. As you recall from Chapter 1, this part of your brain is not fully functional until you are in your mid-twenties.

When you, as an adult, are anxious, agitated, or emotionally numb, there is less blood flow to your prefrontal lobes. Your threat system has taken over. When you are distressed, you need to be reassured and calmed; otherwise, you risk throwing a fit like a toddler does. Deep breathing is so helpful here. Intentional breathing activates the parasympathetic nervous system, which calms the threat system and restores reasoning capacity.

When you are upset, treat yourself in the same way a loving mother responds to her young child. She hugs, kisses, cleanses with a warm washcloth, distracts, rocks, sings soothing songs, and does whatever else she can think of. Your adult mind and body needs comforting attention, too. It is a common misunderstanding to think that adults should shrug off, get over, or suck up emotional distress. It is more beneficial to give yourself the loving parent treatment than to comfort in ways that are detrimental, which is what happens when you soothe with carbohydrates, alcohol, drugs, overwork, and shopping.

Review ways that you comfort your child. If you do not have a child, review ways that kind relatives and friends comfort their children.

Practice ....

Ways to Comfort Yourself

In the space below, write about how you and/or loved ones comfort children. Which of these ways would help comfort you?

_____

_____

_____

_____

_____

_____

When Breathing Does Not Calm—Something Else Does

Being able to emotionally regulate yourself is so important when you begin to engage with emotions that I briefly address stabilization skills again here. Remember, it is healing to tenderly care for emotions and not healing to slide into old, painful emotional pools.

At times, breathing does not calm. When your breath is shallow and heart rate is fast, you may experience discomfort when focusing on breathing. Also, when you feel numb, breath may not be a helpful focus, at least initially.

There are other ways to calm, as discussed in Chapter 3. Here is a brief review.

- A second way is to become more present in the body by pressing both feet down on the floor. This can help, especially when feeling numb or overwhelmed.
- A third way is to concentrate on what you see in the immediate area around you. This can help when fear of the future or sadness over the past arises. You cannot concentrate on here and now and pay attention to elsewhere.
- A fourth way is to move your body. Stand up and stretch. This can interrupt focus on emotional discomfort.

After interrupting your attention with one of these methods, you may benefit from taking a few intentional breaths to engage your nervous system's relaxation response.

Practice ....

Repeating Emotional Stabilization Skills

It takes much repetition to learn new skills, including emotional stabilization skills. Try each of the following on one more time.

- Press your feet into the floor.
- Slowly look around the room. Name three things you see.
- Stand up. Stretch and move your body.
- Take a few intentional breaths.

Journal about your experience as a way to reinforce your skills.

_____

_____

_____

_____

Being There for Yourself—Take a Vow

In good times and bad times, you need support. Thanks to your affiliation system, you benefit tremendously from being supported when you are sad, afraid, or angry. Although you need to seek and accept assistance from others, you also need to learn to be there for yourself.

Other people are not always available to you, whereas you are always available to yourself. Plus, incredible strength comes from being a reliable friend to yourself. When you become your own best friend, you have an intimate source of support within. Someone is there for you wherever you go. With practice, your inner conversation becomes friendly and you feel less alone. You become acclimated to being encouraged, which makes it easier to be in supportive relationships with others.

Vows matter. Plan to make one with yourself, similar to a marriage vow—a commitment to be there for yourself in health and sickness, for better and worse, until your death. Imagine making the following promises to yourself. You will not abandon yourself during tough times, you will celebrate successes, you will be compassionate with yourself, and you will cultivate happiness.

This commitment to be your own best friend is not self-indulgent. This promise to be there for yourself is as sacred as a marriage vow. It does require that you recognize that your life matters and that you desire to cultivate loving neuronal pathways. Do this for your sake and for the sake of others you care about.

Practice ....

Making a Vow to Be There For Yourself

Vows involve symbols and ritual. Select a ring or other piece of jewelry that represents your oath to yourself. Decide on time and location. Choose a beautiful place that feels well suited for conducting a ceremony. Plan to say a vow, read a poem, listen to a song, light a candle, or do whatever else suits you.

Use the space below for preliminary planning. Identify time and location, select a symbol, write a rough draft of a vow. If ready, make a statement of commitment to be there for yourself.

_____

_____

_____

_____

_____

Treating Distress with Mercy

Given harsh societal attitudes about emotions, it is understandable if you are severe with yourself with regard to your emotions. Cultural attitudes become internalized and go unquestioned. Much of this occurs in the unconscious. As a result, like many people, you may unwittingly clamp down on emotions in general, not just the ones that overwhelm you or are undesired.

You probably don't share distress with people who are harsh with you. Generally, you don't feel as emotionally safe with them and thus avoid the possibility of being scolded by them. As a result, they do not get to know you intimately. The same may be true in your relationship with yourself. If you shun emotional vulnerability out of habit, because you were taught to hold yourself together or told to keep secrets, you don't really get to know yourself. Furthermore, and equally important, you miss the opportunity to open your heart for yourself. Much is gained, including the capacity to feel compassion for yourself, by becoming conscious of emotions.

Practicing mercy is an important skill for tending to painful emotions. *Mercy* is defined as showing compassion toward someone you have the power to punish or harm. Obvious examples are a parent offering kindness when a distressed child misbehaves and a boss gently acknowledging an employee's error.

It takes training and practice to learn to treat emotions with mercy. Use the acronym MERCY to help you remember the sequence.

M—Meet. A first step is to meet your emotion. Picture opening a door and greeting an emotion. Say "Hello, my anxiety," "Hello, my sadness," or "Hello, my irritation" as a gesture of acknowledgment. Breathe. Give yourself credit, as this is the opposite of pushing an emotion away.

E—Engage. A second step is to engage your emotion. Picture yourself being curious and calm. Say "Tell me a little about yourself." Breathe, observe, and listen to what your emotion says so you can better understand it. This is a mindful and kind relationship between you as observer and you as experiencer of emotion.

R—Respond. A third step is to respond to your emotion. Picture yourself offering compassion. Say "I hear you, I am with you." Breathe and offer gentle support. Fear needs reassurance to calm it, sadness needs comfort to lighten it, and irritation needs understanding to soothe it. Offer words like "It's okay; we'll get through this together" to anxiety. Whisper words like "This is so hard; one breath and one day at a time. I am with you" to sadness. Say words like "This seems unfair; I am sorry. I am here for you" to irritation.

C—Calm. A fourth step is to calm your body. Breathe, walk, stretch, feel your feet on the floor, or otherwise gently attend to your body. You felt your emotions in your body. Now give yourself a little tender care.

Y—Yes! A fifth step is to say "Yes!" You let yourself feel your emotions. Notice the sense of aliveness, of authenticity. Express gratitude. Celebrate. Reinforce your skill set. You walked on a newer neuronal pathway. You turned toward life by allowing yourself feel more fully human.

Practice ....

Offering MERCY to an Emotion

M—Meet an emotion. Write a greeting. Acknowledge some emotion. Start with something small that does not overwhelm.

_____

_____

_____

E—Engage this emotion. Get to know it. Ask about it. Write a response from this emotion to you. Read what it says to you.

_____

_____

_____

R—Respond to this emotion. Write some words to this emotion from the wise, peaceful you.

_____

_____

_____

C—Calm your body. Move your body, take a few big breaths, stretch. Now write some words describing what you did to take care of yourself.

_____

_____

_____

Y—Yes! Celebrate your practice. Express gratitude. Be a cheerleader for yourself. Write some words to commemorate your efforts.

_____

_____

_____

Being There for Grief

Grief is unavoidable. If you live long enough, you encounter grief, the often-dreaded experience of loss, longing, regrets, letting go, and eventually, reorganizing. Sorrow has its own stages, with shock, denial, anger, depression, and acceptance in the mix. This process takes time, beginning with the all-consuming early phase. Powerful grief can be likened to swimming in unrelenting ocean waves that toss you ashore, then pull you back out. After being thrashed around for some time, you do learn to take deep breaths and dive below the big waves. Blessedly, the waves of grief eventually become calmer.

You don't forget significant losses, and you are changed by them. Grief leaves two life-altering insights. One is recognition of the precious, transient nature of life and the other is profound knowing of the importance of love. When grief is thwarted, these insights may be suppressed. Their emergence results from compassionately being there for grief.

Grief is about much more than the loss of loved ones. It arises as you tend to unworthiness and emotional maltreatment. You grieve for yourself and others, for what you missed out on and the significant impacts maltreatment had on you and loved ones. When you look deeply, you see how innocent you were and how unconscious, unhealed, and even innocent others were. You truly understand the power of interpersonal neurobiology, and you grow in compassion.

Moving through grief is more possible when you meet it with mindfulness and mercy. Mindfulness reassures you that you can breathe, you can go moment by moment, you can focus on small steps, and you can practice kindness. When grief comes, be gentle and seek support. Remember that we all experience grief. You are not alone in your grief even though it may seem like you are.

Practice ....

Offer MERCY To a Small Grief

Be very gentle here. Bring to mind a memory of a loss, one that may be tender but not overwhelming. Remember you are practicing. Write a few words to acknowledge the memory.

_____

_____

_____

_____

Practice MERCY and breathe.

M—Meet this small grief. Write a greeting. Acknowledge some emotion. Start with something small that does not overwhelm.

_____

_____

_____

E—Engage this small grief. Get to know it. Ask what it has to say. Write a response from this emotion. Read what it says.

_____

_____

_____

R—Respond to this grief. Write some words to this emotion from the wise, peaceful you.

_____

_____

_____

C—Calm your body. Move your body, take a few big breaths, stretch. Describe what you did to take care of yourself.

_____

_____

_____

Y—Yes! Celebrate your practice. Express gratitude. Be a cheerleader for yourself. Write some words to commemorate your efforts.

_____

_____

_____

Comfort Pose and Self-Love Mantra

The importance of cultivating a loving relationship with yourself cannot be overemphasized. You deserve and need reliable self-care. This is true for everyone and even more so when you have been shamed, shunned, violated, or bullied. In the aftermath of trauma, your frightened nervous system needs a steady hand to hold on to. Treating yourself with love affirms your goodness. Taking tender care of yourself is not selfish; it is redemptive and makes you more available to others.

Comfort pose is an easy, adaptable, and simple posture. Sit comfortably. Place one hand on your belly and one hand over your heart. Adjust as desired. For example, you could hold both hands over your heart, hold your opposite arms in a hug, or rest your cheek in one arm. Touch your body in a way that connects and sooths. If easier, hug a pillow. Rock for a minute, be aware of breathing, let yourself center and quiet. Then repeat a self-love mantra, such as "My dear, I am here. I am learning to take care of you" (mantra inspired by the teachings of Thich Nhat Hahn).

Modify the mantra so that it pleases you. A self-love mantra reinforces your vow to be there for yourself. Repeat the same mantra day after day, and you create a new neuronal pathway in your brain. Practice daily, and you change your life.

Practice ....

Experiencing Self-Love Mantra

Sit in your favorite chair. Place one hand on your belly and one hand over your heart, or hug a pillow. Breathe and calm. Feel the contact of your hands with your body. Silently recite, "My dear, I am here. I am learning to take care of you" (or the self-love mantra of your choosing). Repeat a few times to embed the message. Sit in this tender position for a few minutes.

CHAPTER 6

Increasing Emotional Resilience and Self-Acceptance

> ### Benefits & Clinician Notes
>
> ✓ Increased memories of human goodness
>
> ✓ Emotional resiliency
>
> ✓ Self-confidence
>
> ✓ Self-acceptance
>
> ✓ More enjoyable relationships with others

Introducing self-compassion practices into my clinical work has benefited many, including those with difficult childhoods who wonder if they will ever be loved. It may take time, but with patience and understanding, people can learn to treat themselves with the regard they have long needed and yearned for. I feel like I witness a miracle when people learn to treat themselves with kindness.

A little psychoeducation and big portions of compassion calm the threat system, turn on the affiliation system, and give hope, as this clinical example highlights. Shirley (not her real name) a kind-hearted, lonely woman, struggled with depression. She had a soft-spoken and gentle manner and wondered why she was neglected in love relationships. Shirley revealed through tidbits that she experienced extreme childhood neglect and maltreatment. It is a wonder that she functioned as well as she did.

I gradually recommended self-compassion practices to her. At first, Shirley reported that they did not work for her. We discussed how kindness confused her threat system, since those who took care of her also hurt her when she was a child. She initially comforted herself by hugging a pillow, then later by cradling herself and rubbing her arms. I encouraged Shirley to list people who had been kind to her, beginning with people in her current life, to remind herself of human goodness. Over time, she could offer metta (taught in this chapter) to her sense of not deserving love. She offered tonglen (also taught in this chapter) to her belief about not being normal, which helped her realize that others with difficult childhoods suffer similarly.

A few years later, Shirley married a man who told her that she was the true love of his life. I see her for infrequent follow-up sessions, and recently she said these words: "I had to wait a long time to be loved, but now I am and I am happy." Shirley credits learning to be kind to herself as a primary benefit of her therapy.

This chapter prepares and then teaches your patients how to treat themselves kindly. In its truest form, self-compassion consists of extending kindness to yourself over and over until compassion becomes central to who you are—until compassion is your first response to suffering within yourself and in others.

This is powerful medication, because, as discussed in Chapter 1, love resolves fear. However, fear can impair your ability to trust love. Accordingly, self-compassion has to approach distrust wisely and respectfully. When the ones who were supposed to be there for you and in many ways did take care of you also hurt you, your ability to trust kindness can be compromised. That may translate into difficulty with self-compassion. Fortunately, love has its ways. This chapter outlines how to approach the pain of not deserving, trusting, or believing in kindness with gentle directness.

Psychoeducation about the human brain is often needed to prepare your patients for self-compassion practices. Gilbert and Chodon (2014) make the following points.

- The human brain is capable of shocking violence and infinite love. War, with its brutal atrocities and heroic sacrifices, illustrate both capacities.

- This is the brain with which we have to live. Our brain was with us at birth and developed in relationship with others.

- The foremost job of our brain is to preserve the life of the body; thus, the primacy of the threat system.

- Our brain is trainable. This fact is what allows for choice, healing, and change.

- The capacity for self-compassion is innate but needs to be developed via modeling and repeated practice.

Learning self-compassion can be compared to learning a new language as an adult. Both require a lot of repetition, exposure, and motivation. However, if you communicated in two languages while growing up, you are bilingual with seemingly little effort. Likewise, if self-compassion was spoken in your childhood home, the practices in this chapter are more for reinforcing and deepening.

I emphasize yet again that memory gravitates toward the negative. As you recall, the threat system unconsciously stores memories involving risk so it can respond quickly to protect your body from injury. Adults with histories of insecure or avoidant attachment may perceive people who intend no harm as unsafe simply because their detection system for danger is leery of others. These patients need training so their brains can detect goodness in others more accurately.

It is crucial to remember that most people are honorable and that good things do happen. Clinically speaking, you may have to wake up the affiliation system before self-compassion is possible. Some of the following practices are intentional reminders of human decency. They aim to restore faith in humanity. They also prepare your patients for the practices of self-compassion that follow.

Self-Compassion—What It Is and Is Not

The affinity toward compassion seems to be innate. Studies by Hamlin and associates (2007) at the University of British Columbia show 6- to 10-month-old babies being more attracted to a puppet that helps another puppet than to one that hinders another one. Also, various studies of toddlers being helpful to strangers indicate that toddlers tend to be altruistic (Warneken & Tomasello, 2009). Whereas the potential to be compassionate seems to be indwelling, the capacity has to be cultivated.

You learn the words, tone of voice, and gestures of compassion as a result of living in a warm atmosphere of compassion. If you were raised in a cooler atmosphere of unpredictability or harshness, your compassion language may be limited. Fortunately, adults can learn a foreign language, at least enough to get by, and you can learn and expand self-compassion. This is good news, because a little self-compassion, where you are intentionally kind to yourself when you suffer, can make all the difference in healing.

You may not be knowledgeable about the benefits of self-compassion. Some people think that it reflects weakness, will make you lazy, is a poor excuse, or simply doesn't make a difference. That is not what recent research reveals. Kristen Neff (2015) found that self-compassion results in more motivation, willingness to learn, emotional resiliency, and improved self-care.

Neff also reported that practicing compassion toward others doesn't translate into directing compassion toward yourself. Moreover, she found that far more people are kind to others than to themselves. This may mean that you, like many of us, need to learn to be a better friend to yourself. To be self-compassionate, you need to talk to yourself the way you would a friend, give yourself some credit, forgive mistakes, cheer yourself on, and use a welcoming voice in your self-talk.

Neff defined self-compassion as having three main components. They are mindfulness, common humanity, and self-kindness.

- First, be mindful of your suffering. Recognize and approach distress rather than avoid, dismiss, minimize, or suppress it. Acknowledge your distress; i.e., silently say, "This is so hard. I am frustrated," when something doesn't go well.
- Second, recognize that others suffer similarly. Say, "Others suffer this way, too," to remind yourself that you are not the only one who feels this kind of distress.
- Third, self-kindness is a supportive message to yourself, expressed through words such as "It's okay, I understand, we'll get through this."

Self-compassion is more comprehensive than this brief description suggests. This is a starting point. Even if you do not initially resonate with the approach to self-compassion described here, please remain open and curious. You will systematically build the skills of self-compassion.

Pema Chodron, a Buddhist nun, deepens the discussion. She lectures about how self-compassion is profound self-acceptance. She describes it as learning to gaze into your inner life through the eyes of understanding and love. Chodron (2013) teaches the following themes in her many books. For the sake of brevity, I simply list them.

- True self-compassion has benefits beyond your relationship with yourself. It transforms your relationships with others.
- Accept yourself, and you are more accepting of others.
- Be kind to yourself, and you are kinder to others.
- Know your own darkness, and you can be there for others during dark times.

Note that self-compassion is not a maneuver to make yourself into an improved you. Some part of you may think that if you just practice self-compassion, you will be fixed up once and for all. You are already good enough. Practicing self-compassion helps you to accept, be understanding toward, and be kind to yourself. The result is that you feel better about yourself.

Practicing self-compassion helps you to experience compassion in the core of who you are. It replaces chronic low self-worth, fear, and sadness, those historical perspectives that can seem so central. Obviously, you don't alter your history; after all, what happened did happen. But you can understand how your history affected you and transform your relationship with your history.

Why Kindness to Self at Times Causes Distress

If you have a history of neglect, maltreatment, or other interpersonal betrayal, your lower brain may be suspicious of kindness. It may respond to compassion, even years later, by activating the threat system. Stephen Porges (2011) writes that abuse history is related to autonomic regulation. This may result in a nervous system that has difficulty relaxing even when there is no immediate threat.

Your brain can become programmed to feel unsafe in close, nurturing relationships, at least to some degree. As a result, you may attract people who reenact the same betrayal you experienced years earlier. Even though you may yearn for kindness, your brain can become wary of it and push it away. If your brain doesn't trust the kindness of others, it may need to be trained to trust self-compassion.

On the other hand, when caretakers provided reliable care, your lower brain, via your vagal nerve—the primary nerve of the parasympathetic nervous system—replies to kindness by activating the relaxation response. You and your affiliation motivational system feel comforted when others support you. Likewise, you and your brain are more able to receive self-compassion.

You may find that the three-part compassion practice presented in the previous section helps you to identify some distrust about self-compassion. You will learn others' practices to ease mistrust shortly.

Practice ·

Exploring Mistrust of Compassion

This is a way to explore and acknowledge mistrust of compassion.

- Sit meditatively for a few minutes. Focus on your breathing. When you feel ready, quietly say the following words:
- "In this moment, I mistrust compassion."
- "Others feel this way also."
- "I offer understanding and support to myself and others who mistrust."

Journal your response to this. Note if mistrusting compassion felt real.

_____

_____

_____

_____

Connecting to Your Heart—Three Simple Practices

The foundation for self-compassion is waking up your affiliation system and/or keeping it awake. How? By pulling up memories of people being there for you and memories of life's beauty. Remember the negativity bias of the brain and how you retain negative memories more than positive ones. Accessing memories of life's goodness balances your perspective of the way life is, helps you hold difficulties in a broader context, and activates your affiliation motivational system.

Following are brain-training practices to remind you of human decency and pave the way for you to treat yourself with compassion.

Practice ···

Who/What Do You Love?

This one focuses on what you love, appreciate, and value. It is designed to connect you to the goodness and sanctity of life. Consider the following in looking at what you love: people, animals, the natural world, spiritual beings, beautiful art, soulful music, heart-touching literature, inspirational movies, and beneficial sciences.

Sit quietly and meditatively for a few minutes. Focus on your breathing. Simply be with yourself. When you feel ready, continue on.

Write your responses to the question. Give specific answers. When you feel finished, search for and list a few more.

Who/what do you love?

_____

_____

_____

_____

_____

_____

_____

What are the effects of this practice?

_____

_____

_____

_____

Practice ....

Who Has Been a Rainbow in Your Life?

Everyone has stormy times. Maya Angelou, a beloved poet and social activist, talked about experiencing many storms but also many rainbows in the form of people who supported her. She would recall everyone who had been nice to her and envision them joining her on stage. She brilliantly modeled the practice of calling on people who have been kind to you to be with you when you need them. Doing so accesses your affiliation system and restores faith in human goodness.

- Sit quietly and meditatively for a few minutes. Focus on your breathing. Simply be with yourself. When you feel ready, continue on.
- List people, animals, and spiritual beings who were there for you during difficult times. This includes people who you knew, as well as strangers who were kind. Add to this list later as memories pop up.

_____

_____

_____

_____

_____

_____

_____

| Practice | .... |

Who Has Seen Your Goodness?

Children experience their worthiness when it is mirrored back to them by adoring family members. Bessel van der Kolk (2015), a leading authority on trauma treatment, teaches that children need to be the apple of their parents' eyes. He adds that the absence of positive mirroring is a damaging and frequent form of child maltreatment.

According to Vincent Felitti and associates (1998), reporting on the Childhood Adversity Study, more than half of U.S. citizens experience childhood maltreatment. Many children do not experience their parent's eyes lighting up often enough. Not feeling treasured takes a huge toll on self-worth. Add verbal, physical, or sexual maltreatment, and it is no wonder that low self-worth is prevalent.

Ideally, you first experience love's gaze at home as a child. However, any gaze that touches your heart, whether from loved ones or strangers, helps you to know your innate worthiness. This is true for children and for adults. Such looks can come in unexpected ways. One woman recalled feeling seen, really for the first time, when she was a young girl and her neighbor looked into her eyes and softly commented that the color of her coat showed off her beautiful hazel eyes.

- Collect memories of times you felt valued by another. Looks are poignant; however, messages about how valuable you are can come in many forms. Perhaps you can recall a sincere compliment, a gift, a soft voice you trusted, or a soothing, respectful touch. Such memories can recede into subconsciousness, so be gentle with yourself if few memories readily come to mind.

- Sit quietly and meditatively for a few minutes. Focus on your breathing. Simply be with yourself. When you feel ready, continue on.

- List experiences when your goodness was seen by others. Add to this list in the future as memories come up.

_____

_____

_____

_____

_____

_____

_____

_____

Teachers of Compassion

As a baby, you required tender care from a responsible adult to stay alive. Diaper changes and frequent milk supply were not enough. There had to be cuddling and skin touch for you to survive. You are alive and reading this, so you received at least some loving care. Optimally, a loving parent developed a deep bond with you and did everything possible to ensure that your needs were met.

Loving parents exemplify the three characteristics of compassion: a loving bond, wisdom, and the aspiration to reduce suffering. The first characteristic of compassion seems obvious: a caring connection. Loving parents give care to their children, because they touch their heart. Second, loving parents understand the cause of a child's discomfort and know how to alleviate it. Finally, caring parents desire to actually do something when their child is suffering.

Skillful parents develop their innate capacity for compassion. Somehow they transformed their life experiences into kindness. Again, the comparison to learning a language is useful. You have to hear others speak it. If it is a language not spoken at home, you may have a mentor, yet you have to do the reading, speaking, and writing to be an effective communicator. The same is true with compassion. It is helpful to have teachers and to practice.

Compassion shows up in many forms and through countless teachers. They are the people, animals, and spiritual beings who care for you. They recognize your distress and its causes and aspire to reduce your pain in direct and indirect ways. These teachers show you how wonderfully compassionate you can be. Many compassion masters are well known, including the following.

- Beloved spiritual beings, including Christ and Buddha.
- Saints, such as St. Theresa, who served the poor in India; St. Catherine of Siena, who devoted herself to relieving mental and emotional suffering in others; and St. Francis of Assisi, who devoted himself to the afflicted and impoverished.
- Political leaders like Mahatma Ghandi, Nelson Mandela, and Martin Luther King, Jr., who practiced nonviolent social action and lifted the consciousness of millions.
- Artists, exemplified by the poet Rumi and the painter and sculptor Michelangelo, whose works reflect the sanctity of human life.
- Heros, such as Oscar Schindler, who sheltered Jews during World War II, and Victor Frankl, a Holocaust survivor who offered hope and dignity to his imprisoned comrades.
- Scientists like Marie Curie who discovered radium used in life-saving x-rays; Jonas Salk, who developed the polio vaccine; and Albert Einstein, whose numerous achievements in physics serve as an inspiration to many.

Lesser-known teachers of compassion are the parents, relatives, neighbors, friends, educators, pets, and strangers who have touched your life with kindness. Unnamed heroes and heroines, they modeled human goodness.

A central practice of self-compassion is gathering up the well-known and unknown teachers of compassion who mentored you. Making this list matters, because doing so warms your affiliation system and reminds you how to be kind to yourself.

Practice ··

Listing Teachers of Compassion

Sit quietly and, meditatively for a few minutes. Focus on your breathing. Simply be with yourself. When you feel ready, continue on.

List well-known public figures whose works were/are infused with compassion. Add to this list over time.

_____

_____

_____

_____

List people and animals who were/are personally compassionate to you. Add to this list over time.

_____

_____

_____

_____

The Voice of the Inner Friend

Everyone would benefit from having a dear friend on the inside who has their best interests at heart and isn't shy about letting them know it. Fortunately, you can create a friend who encourages you, challenges you, holds you accountable to your ethics and goals, greets you with a smile, forgives mistakes, and cheers you on. Cultivating this intimate friend not only emotionally uplifts you, it helps to generate beneficial neurotransmitters. Why not release a little dopamine, associated with pleasure and reward, and some oxytocin, associated with relationship bonding and contentment?

The voice of the inner friend does not condemn, accuse, or sound vile and harsh. However, sometimes the inner critic's voice is disguised as a helpful voice that instead causes fear and anger and amps up cortisol, a hormone released in response to stress. A voice that attacks personal worth and reinforces unworthiness does not need to be cultivated. It does need big doses of understanding. You have opportunity to give compassion to the inner critic later in this chapter.

According to Kristen Neff (2015), most people speak more kindly to others than to themselves. Training is often required for you talk to yourself in a friendly manner. Gilbert and Chodon (2014) recommend that you begin your schooling by finding your friendly voice, which you can do momentarily. As a way to begin, acknowledge the following.

- Friends communicate with each other in cordial, optimistic, and consoling tones.
- Friends on the outside are not always available, unlike the inner friend, who, once cultivated, is ever with you.
- Your wellbeing depends on you being your own companion.
- Your brain is capable of remarkable change. Becoming more of a friend to yourself is possible with practice.

Practice ....

Using the Voice of a Friend When Speaking to Yourself

Sit quietly and meditatively for a few minutes. Focus on your breathing. Simply be with yourself. When you feel ready, continue on. So what if you feel silly? You are learning a life changing skill.

Greet yourself, out loud. Using a friendly voice, say, "Hello, [your name], I am happy to see you." Repeat!

Cheer yourself on, out loud. Using a friendly voice, say, "[your name], you can do this; hang in there; remember it's one step at a time." Repeat!

Hold yourself accountable, out loud. Using a friendly voice, say, "[your name], you know this is important to you, so do what you have to do. Come on, you will feel better." Repeat!

Forgive a mistake, out loud. Using a friendly voice, say, "[your name], I know you feel bad; everyone makes mistakes. You are learning. I am ever on your side. I love you, and I forgive you." Repeat!

Celebrate a success, out loud. Using a friendly voice, say, "[your name], I am so proud of you—that is awesome. You did it, way to go." Repeat!

Journal about this practice. Use your friendly voice as you write about the experience and what you discovered.

_____

_____

_____

Three-Part Self-Compassion Note

Continue your schooling, and over time the practices of self-compassion change the way you encounter yourself. You begin to experience yourself as being kind hearted, and more of the time you respond to unworthiness, depression, and anxiety with tender loving care.

So far, you have explored your teachers of compassion, reviewed experiences of receiving compassion, and practiced cultivating the voice of an inner friend. A next step is writing a note in which you respond to sadness, anxiety, or low self-esteem with compassion. The idea is to write, in the voice of your inner best friend, to your distress. This three-part format, inspired by the teachings of Gilbert and Chodon (2014), offers a straightforward way of writing such a note.

- Kindly recognize and approach. Write a sentence acknowledging your distress. Example: "Hello. I know that you are afraid to speak to the group and worry that you will mess up and look inept."

- Kindly guide and be present. Write a sentence offering practical support. Example: "You can do this. Jot down your ideas, take a few deep breaths, and remember previous successes."

- Kindly appreciate and mirror goodness. Write a sentence expressing admiration. Example: "I admire your willingness to show up. You are sensitive, funny, curious, and big hearted."

Practice ···

Writing Notes of Compassion to Yourself

Sit quietly and meditatively for a few minutes. Focus on your breathing. Simply be with yourself. When you feel ready, continue on.

Write at least two notes of compassion to yourself. It may take a little practice to feel comfortable with this, especially if this is a new skill for you.

_____

_____

_____

_____

_____

_____

_____

Metta Prayer—Offering Loving Kindness to Any Inner Aspect that Feels Not Deserving

Amazingly, there is a way to support the aspect of you that does not feel deserving of kindness. According to Christopher Germer (2009), you can offer it well wishes. Dishonored, discarded aspects inevitably yearn for kindness. The following prayer of loving kindness bypasses undeserving and is received by yearning.

Metta prayer is a sending of well wishes to yourself and others. *Metta*, a Pali word, means loving kindness, friendliness, or good will. There are many versions of this prayer. Following is a simple one that you can modify for your purposes.

> *May you be happy.*
> *May you be safe.*
> *May you be well.*
> *May you be at peace.*

As a beginning practice, offer this prayer to someone you care about. Visualize their face, say their name, and sincerely send well wishes to them. Now, offer this prayer to yourself.

Below is an abbreviated metta prayer that you can offer to any inner aspect of undeserving. Explore this when you feel ready. This practice may feel tender.

Practice ···

Offering Metta to Sense of Undeserving

1. Center your awareness in your body. Breathe, touch your heart, or feel your feet on the floor.

2. Recall a compassion teacher or a memory of someone who valued you to help you tap into compassion.

3. Gently acknowledge any sense of undeserving inside yourself.

4. In a loving voice, say, "May you be happy, may you experience peace" to that disheartened inner aspect. Softly repeat a few times.

Sit quietly for a few moments.

Journal what this practice was like for you. What did you notice?

Metta Prayer—Compassion for the Inner Critic

Martin Luther King, Jr. preached that meeting hatred with hatred does not resolve anything. Hatred has to be approached with love for healing to occur. Accordingly, the scorn, scolding, and unrelenting attacks of the inner critic need to be approached with understanding and from just a little distance away, so you can breathe and tap into compassion. The inner critic cannot be locked in a closet or driven out like a venomous snake. The inner critic warrants respect and care, but it is only open to a certain kind of care—not self-love mantras or "touchy-feely" stuff. As Gilbert and Chodon (2014) wrote, by its nature, the inner critic ridicules and resists compassion.

The inner critic was discussed in Chapter 4. You practiced naming it, understanding it, and using a hand gesture to create a little space from it. To review, raise your hand in a firm, kind gesture while calmly saying "Not now" to interrupt it. This momentarily quiets its voice.

Your hand up in the "Not now" gesture buys you a moment. Take a breath and lift your other hand to your heart. Here you are with one hand in the air gently keeping the inner critic at bay and the other hand over your heart in contact with kindness. Visualize the inner critic off to your side if you like. Use a kind voice to extend metta to the inner critic. Say words such as "May you be at peace. May you be safe," to offer the kind of support it understands.

You may need to practice this many times daily. Each practice calms your nervous system, grows your capacity to respond to the inner critic, and allows the inner critic to become more dormant.

Practice ....

Offering Metta to Your Inner Critic

Be gentle and go easy. Learn this practice when you are calm and feel ready.

Call your inner critic by name. Lift one hand up and say "Not now." Draw your other hand to your heart. Center, breathe, and then looking toward your extended hand, send wishes of peace and safety to the inner critic. Remain focused on you as the compassionate one. Take a couple of breaths.

Journal your response to this practice.

_____

_____

_____

_____

Tonglen Practice—Receiving Suffering and Sending Compassion

You can unlock your capacity to love yourself, and you can change your life from the inside out. As a famous quote by Mahatma Ghandi proclaims, "You must be the change you want to see." Give sincerity, understanding, and kindness to yourself, and they radiate outward, touching others and enhancing the greater good.

This next practice helps you feel connected with others. Pema Chodron (2013) writes of the importance of accepting our shared humanity through suffering but also, and especially, through compassion. Considering interpersonal neurobiology, inclusiveness makes perfect sense.

Tonglen helps you to feel our shared humanity by approaching it in your inner life. For example, by gently taking in your unworthiness, you recognize unworthiness in others. By touching fear in yourself, you know fear in others, and by feeling sadness in yourself, you understand it in others. In this way, you realize that the emotional and mental pain that feels so terribly personal and isolating is actually a shared experience.

Tonglen is a practice of opening your heart to suffering and giving compassion to yourself and others who suffer similarly. For example, you can take in your unworthiness and send compassion to yourself and others who have low self-worth. Likewise, you can receive fear and give compassion. You can breathe in sadness and breathe out compassion. Compassion for yourself and others grows, and you discover an overflowing reservoir of kindness that is larger than you.

Gilbert and Chodon (2014) describe Tonglen as a central practice in healing shame and depression. This makes sense because shame and depression are so disconnecting and isolating.

Taking suffering into your heart and sending compassion to it is an act of goodness that restores human dignity and human connection.

Tonglen is often practiced in rhythm with breathing. It goes something like this: "Breathing in, I am aware of my suffering and know that others suffer like me. Breathing out, I send loving kindness to myself and others who suffer like me." This helps you touch into suffering without becoming lost in it, because one moment you approach it and a moment later, you shift into compassion. You breathe in suffering and breathe out compassion.

Practice ....

Practicing Tonglen

Sit quietly and meditatively for a few minutes. Focus on your breathing. Simply be with yourself. When you feel ready, continue on.

Start gently. Begin this practice with some small irritation or ache, perhaps a frustration with a task or a headache, so that you do not become overly upset while learning.

1. Breathing in, I am aware of [name your suffering].
2. And I know others suffer like me.
3. Breathing out, I send loving kindness to myself and others who suffer like this.

Select another small example of suffering and repeat. When you feel ready, after many repetitions, practice Tonglen with bigger examples of suffering, such as low self-worth, anxiety, or depression. You may choose to continue with this practice for 5 to 10 minutes.

Journal about your experience with Tonglen.

_____

_____

_____

_____

_____

_____

CHAPTER 7

Healing Unworthiness and Shame

Benefits & Clinician Notes

✓ Learning about the causes of unworthiness to undo self-blame

✓ Understanding the ways unworthiness and shame live in body and mind

✓ Releasing the imprint of shame in the body

✓ Recognizing "not enough" as identity and creating space around it

✓ Inquiring into new narrative

✓ Exploring true values

Working with people who do not know their own goodness usually melts my heart. Often, they respect life and don't hurt others, yet they do not know how lovely they are. Slowly, with the help of brain knowledge and psychoeducation, mindfulness interventions, self-compassion, trauma-informed yoga, and the winds of grace, they begin to experience their worth. Witnessing their transformations fills me with wonder and gratitude.

The following is an example. I had the privilege of working with Cynthia (not her real name) for a year. We were both deeply touched by how her inner experience and perception of herself changed during that time.

Cynthia came to my office trembling with anxiety. A hard-working professional, she exhausted herself in her efforts to do good. When growing up, she was not positively mirrored enough, was pushed into adult responsibilities, was criticized more than encouraged at home, and was isolated from relatives she adored. Cynthia was bright and generous. By the time she was a teenager, other adults began taking her under their wing. People beyond her family saw her radiance. However, the imprint of not being enough had taken root.

A first turning point in therapy was when Cynthia discovered that she felt safe while resting in the legs up the wall yoga pose (taught in this chapter). Another turning point in therapy was when Cynthia practiced listing people who saw her goodness. To her surprise, she remembered significant relationships long forgotten. Yet another turning point was permitting herself to take care of herself, release perfectionism, and ask for help in response to a health issue.

And a life-altering turning point was when she began questioning unworthiness as her primary identity. She understood how "not feeling good enough" developed in her personality and that she had been conditioned to not know her goodness, an insight she grasped intellectually before sensing in her heart.

At the closing session, Cynthia talked about how anxiety and unworthiness still show up at times. Temporarily, she falls back into believing she is a "not-enough" person. Then she has to remind herself that she was born being enough and is enough, just because. Said another way, Cynthia is a worthy human with a historical identity that does not acknowledge her inherent value.

First, some perspective about unworthiness: It is inconceivable that anyone is born with a conscious desire to not like themselves. It is also important to understand that it does not arise of its own accord.

When your patients talk about feeling unworthy, you know that this is not an identity they created autonomously. Forming an identity is linked to interpersonal neurobiology that includes family, community, and culture. Also, inferiority is experienced individually and is shared by groups. For example, someone with a disability may suffer individually and along with others with disabilities who are also marginalized.

Rarely is one individual solely responsible for damaging the sense of worth in another, even when it seems to be so. Something happened that drove the hurtful person to cause harm to another. Some underlying force, and often more than one, contributed. On inquiry, you are apt to uncover a history of transgenerational maltreatment, societal biases such as racism, and/or severe mental illness or addiction.

Unworthiness usually takes root during childhood when identity is forming. Identity, the kind of person you think you are, is truly malleable, which is important to consider because identity can seem so solid. Even as an adult, an unfortunate experience of maltreatment at home or work may cause you to question your basic value.

Experiencing unworthiness can also be an outcome of making tragic and harmful mistakes, the kind that are associated with alcohol, drugs, brain washing, and war. Go against your moral code or offend cultural mores and you and/or society are likely to claim that you are not a good person.

Your patients are more likely to say, "I am too hard on myself," "I feel embarrassed about my inadequacies," "I feel nervous just being me," or "I have low self-esteem," rather than say, "I suffer from unworthiness." They are even less likely to say, "I suffer from shame." Shame is a strong word that is not easy to associate with yourself. Even saying the word can feel embarrassing.

In this chapter, the words shame and unworthiness are used together. They coexist even though there is a telling distinction between them. Shame relates more to the body. It is a painful feeling of humiliation associated with intense sympathetic nervous system activation and feelings of powerlessness. Unworthiness is more of the mind and describes the kind of person you think you are. The word unworthiness means beneath the dignity of or undeserving of and defines lack of merit in character. Shame and unworthiness merge together into a body/mind experience that is a painfully felt sense of self. Your patient is apt to think that they are an unworthy person (narrative describing lack of value) who feels ashamed (bodily experience of humiliation) of who they are.

The mixture of shame and unworthiness is a paralyzing body/mind experience of being not good enough. Enough is the operative word. Occasionally, people feel like they are "80 percenters," almost smart or lovable. Some compensate for a deep down feeling of inadequacy by overachieving. Others live with low-level depression, and more than a few know self-loathing.

Shame and unworthiness are rarely identified as reasons for seeking mental health services, whereas low self-esteem is, as is being disappointed with the self. Few people go around saying, "I am a person of low merit," or "I feel so ashamed." They just compare themselves negatively with others, feel anxious about who they are, and don't feel deserving of the wonderful things in life.

The greatest healing for unworthiness is discovering that human life is sacred. Unworthiness as an identity is an innocent misunderstanding. Any belief in who you are that does not reflect inherent dignity misses the mark of your true identity. When I interviewed him in 1999, Father Thomas Keating, who popularized Centering Prayer, said, "Low self-esteem results from not knowing who you are," (NurrieStearns, 1999). Unlike guilt, which is feeling bad about some behavior, unworthiness goes to the core of identity. It's not that you are guilty of making a mistake; it's that you are a mistake. Healing is about reclaiming your true identity even if and when cultural and familial forces that devalue you persist.

Your patients may benefit by going through this chapter with your support. This material may be evocative even as it relieves. Your knowledge helps your patients review learned unworthiness without collapsing into it. Your skills help them understand and relieve shame. Your presence helps them stay in present moment awareness, and you seeing them as worthy mirrors their innate dignity back to them.

Causes of Unworthiness and Shame

The information in this section is familiar. Many of the causes live in collective and familial unconsciousness and are experienced as "just the way it is." The purpose of reviewing these causes is to raise your consciousness about forces that impact your own life.

Societal Attitudes and Institutionalized Oppression

Unworthiness and shame feel horribly individual yet are not. They reflect the social brain that begins with enduring societal forces and includes institutionalized beliefs, laws, and policies. Any discussion of them must begin with collective forces that oppress groups of people. Judith Herman (1992) a groundbreaker in the field of trauma, argued that psychological trauma can be understood only in a social context.

Consider long-held stigmas that devalue others. Obvious examples include racism, poverty, misogyny/prejudice against women, xenophobia/fear of foreigners, ableism/prejudice against disabled, stigma against LBGTQ, and religious discrimination. If you are born as a person of color, a woman, a queer person, someone with a mental or physical disability, someone in poverty, or a person who experiences discrimination based on your ethnicity or religion, you are persecuted by cultural biases. The damaging power of these societal forces cannot be overemphasized. It is true that progress in human rights is being made; however, attitudes and policies are slow to change.

Whereas these forces impinge on people, not all oppressed persons suffer low self-worth. The fact that they don't highlights the extraordinary human capacity to live with love and dignity in the midst of cultural disadvantage.

Family Heritage

The term *transgenerational psychic umbilical cord* refers to beliefs and lifestyles passed down from one generation to the next. Religious orientation, educational and occupational opportunity, gender roles, racial and ethnic stigmas, language, and expression of violence and compassion are modeled by adults and absorbed by developing brains. The examples are endless. When grandmother is embittered by poverty, hard work, and few pleasures, she may unwittingly scold her granddaughter for attempting to make a better life. A man who witnessed his dad treating his mother unkindly may unthinkingly treat his wife and daughter with disrespect. Looking through this lens of understanding, you see how those who influenced you were impacted by generations before them.

You can heal and pass along a more loving heritage. However, you do need to recognize engrained tendencies and meet them with understanding when they inevitably resurface.

Mental Illness, Devastating Trauma, and Substance Addictions in Parents

No one desires mental illness, dangerous addiction, or life-altering trauma. However, these experiences are prevalent, and they impact children. These forces can unconsciously cause parents to neglect, scare, and abuse children and not know how much harm their behavior causes. Children may end up ashamed of their parents, frightened for their safety, wondering what is wrong, and wishing to live with a "normal" family. Often, children don't like to talk about what goes on at home and may be told that what happens there is nobody else's business: Being secretive is the norm. One woman talked about how her family looked normal to others—appearing okay was important. For most of her life, she felt terribly insecure, but she looked great.

If your self-worth was dimmed by these forces, know that you can reclaim a sense of dignity. Understanding and self-compassion go a long way toward restoring your inner light.

Neighborhood, School, Church, and Work

Schoolyard bullies, mean-spirited teachers, abusive clergy, mentally unstable neighbors, and harsh bosses can be cruel, sexually mistreat, verbally abuse, threaten, emotionally manipulate, and trick you into doubting your memory or perceptions. Minorities, women, queer people, the disabled, immigrants, and people who are poor are at higher risk of being targeted. Often, the abuser has more authority or physical strength, and the person being mistreated is more vulnerable. When you are treated disrespectfully, you may begin feel disgraced and over time believe that you are a disgrace. Being treated inhumanely puts you at risk of developing low self-worth.

Shortly, you will learn how to lift the stain of mistreatment into the light of understanding, which helps to restore your human dignity.

Horrible Events

Sometimes, terrible things, such as automobile crashes, war, and industrial accidents, happen. We humans are relational, and incidents involving people that maim or take life are often a blow to personal dignity. Briefly bow to the soldier who feels ashamed of firing his gun on civilians, the mother who feels mortified that she could not protect her child, and the construction worker who is horrified that he couldn't rescue his trapped coworker. Understandably, such events are tough to deal with and can put you up against your sense of morality. Difficult feelings may arise in response to things others have done and also in response to things for which you feel responsible or may have done; for example, most people would feel terrible if they had killed a pedestrian while driving drunk even if it was an accident.

Acting against your morality or blaming yourself for something unpreventable often puts you in a personal hell. Forgiveness, redemptive actions, and deep understanding are needed. If you blame yourself for something you couldn't prevent, acknowledge both your sense of responsibility and your lack of intent. Give mega doses of mercy and compassion to your pain. You can find healing even after such circumstances.

If you harmed another, quietly admit it. Look deeply into the forces that contributed to your behavior and vow to honor the sanctity of life by making life around you better in some form. This may be a daunting task, but doing so is far better than letting shame eat you alive. You are not alone in your circumstances. St. Francis, beloved for his reverence toward animals, became a peace-loving, compassionate saint after leaving his life as a mercenary in the Crusades.

Practice ··

A Healing Analogy

You can reclaim worth. Although healing requires resolve, putting in effort beats believing a lie of unworthiness. Consider this: A cup of salt in a quart of water makes the water undrinkable, yet a cup of salt in a swimming pool is imperceptible. The same is true for unworthiness. Held secretly within yourself, it damages. When exposed, then released into the light of understanding, unworthiness is diffused. You begin to recognize unworthiness as a historical sense of self that no longer defines you, as an old narrative that you lived through.

In the practice below, you recognize causes of worthiness so they can be held in understanding.

After a little reflection, journal briefly about the causes of unworthiness and shame that you experienced as a way to become more aware. Be gentle—you are looking for understanding, that is all.

Family-of-origin patterns:

_____

_____

_____

Mental illness, substance addiction, and trauma:

_____

_____

_____

Societal attitudes:

_____

_____

_____

The community:

_____

_____

_____

Horrible events:

_____

_____

_____

Words that Humiliate and Degrade

Words that devalue others are not funny, and people who protest being called derogatory names are not overly sensitive. Degrading words can cut into your identity as a worthy being in the same way that a poisonous spider bites into healthy flesh.

Such words often pertain to long-held societal attitudes, especially regarding femininity and masculinity. A brief look at femininity first. The following words and concepts are associated with being feminine in this culture: *domestic, nice, modest, thin, using resources to invest in appearance*, and *having few sexual partners*. Women are often put down with words about being too masculine, ambitious, sexual, and unattractive.

Then, there is body shaming, which is rampant, according to a national eating disorders website. The majority of women see their own bodies through critical eyes and also harshly judge other women's bodies. Some men say hurtful things that either reduce women to being sex objects and/or compare them to idealized body types, which is one aspect of sexism. What's more, these attitudes about femininity impact people of all genders—not just women.

Now a brief look at masculinity. The following words and phrases are considered masculine in this culture: *winning, having emotional control, dominant, pursuing status, powerful,* and *capable of violence.* Men are degraded with words about being too weak, not ambitious enough, or too feminine. How demeaning this is to men! Like the words and concepts that harm women, these attitudes about masculinity impact people of all genders—not just men.

Words that express disdain toward immigrants, people of color, people with disabilities, and queer people are deeply and personally wounding. This kind of talk represents a societal and an individual assault on human rights.

Practice ....

Naming Words That Belittle Others

Write down a few words that you hear being used in this culture to belittle others. Be gentle—you are looking for understanding, that is all.

_____

_____

_____

_____

The Physiology of Shame

Shame is first and foremost a nervous system response. Inevitably, it shows up in physiology and posture. Here is why: Words that insult and those that threaten physical assault affect the nervous system in similar ways. Obviously, a physical strike can result in physical injury. However, verbal abuse feels like a punch to the belly. Both are onslaughts that activate a fight, flight, freeze/feign dead response. Just think about the potential long-lasting effects on someone who is repeatedly devalued.

The body's classic shame response is submission, which is generally adaptive and can even be lifesaving. These are autonomic responses, not ones that are thought out, as your nervous system takes charge of preserving your life. Consider slaves who submitted to plantation owners. Their yielding decreased beatings if they were fortunate.

Submission shows up as body posture in what Ogden and Fisher (2015) describe as a classic shame stance. It is typified by shallow breathing, bowed head, hunched shoulders, downward gaze, an inability to speak, and a wish to be invisible. It is accompanied by flushing, sweating, and racing heartbeat, which are classic signs of sympathetic nervous system activation. Having the head tilted down narrows vision, and having slumped shoulders shrinks body stature and inhibits diaphragmatic breathing. Gut-wrenching images of this posture are seen in movies depicting slaves being sold at auction.

At times, men may respond to oppression more with a fear/defiance mix and alternate between fighting to undo loss of face and avoiding conflict. Their bodies are agitated and ready to fight. This posture is called "angry stance" and shows up as a body that is alert and prepared to pounce. Feet are placed wider than hip distance apart, arms are crossed, muscles are tense, jaw is set, breath is shallow, attention is alert, and eyes stare or scan for danger. Look at pictures of gang members to see this response.

The way shame lives in the body is often unconsciously perpetuated for years.

Practice ....

Exploring a Posture of Shame

Recall a time when you felt mildly shamed or humiliated. Journal about your body's response. Undeniably, shame leaves an unconscious fear imprint. What was your posture like? Did you experience the classic shame stance? Did you experience angry defiance?

_____

_____

_____

_____

Differentiating Among Shame, Defiance, and Noble Postures

Classic shame posture and fear/defiant posture are imprinted in the nervous system and musculature as a result of jolting or repeated exposure to degradation. They continue on as a form of procedural memory in the same way that your body automatically remembers how to ride a bike once it knows how. How your threat system responded to being degrading can remain active even when you are in a safe place surrounded by supportive people.

In contrast, "nobility posture" reflects peace and dignity. It is upright but not rigid. Muscles are responsive, not stiff or limp, and move fluidly. Shoulders are wide and relaxed. Nervous system is calm, and mind is attentive and quiet.

You can teach your body to differentiate among the postures of classic shame, fear/defiance, and nobility. Become aware of what has lived on as habit, and over time, you can intentionally change your body's postural tendency. Your mind begins to follow suit, since body and mind live in close relationship.

Practice ··

Trying On the Postures of Shame, Defiance and Nobility

First, stand in the classic shame posture. Place your feet together, bow your head, slump your shoulders, and gaze at the floor. Notice that your visual field is limited and down. Consider the thoughts, such as "I'm not enough" and "I don't matter," that accompany this posture.

Shake your body to release the posture.

Second, stand in the fear/defiance posture. Place your feet wider than your hips, cross your arms or place your hands on the sides of your waist, tighten your shoulders, and look straight ahead or slightly away with steely eyes. Notice that your visual field is fixed and narrow. Consider the thoughts, such as "Don't mess with me" and "Back off," that accompany this posture.

Shake your body to release the posture.

Third, stand in the noble posture. Place your feet hip distance apart, gently lengthen your spine, softly lift your heart, and relax your shoulders. Gaze comfortably ahead. Notice that your visual field is wide. Consider the thoughts, such as "I'm okay," "I am comfortable," and "I can approach others," that accompany this posture.

Walk around the room experimenting with a tall spine, a lifted heart, and relaxed shoulders. Let your breath be easy. Look around and notice colors and objects. Come back to a seated pose and re-establish nobility in your posture. This pleasant posture reflects innate human dignity.

Journal about your experience of trying on these postures.

_____

_____

_____

_____

Simple Yoga for Healing Physiology of Shame

If you experience unworthiness or shame, your nervous system needs your support. Helping it relax is a major component of healing. A leader in the treatment of trauma, Peter Levine (2015) advocates corrective experiences to retrain your nervous system and your physical movement patterns. Yoga can be a rehabilitative practice that gradually and comfortably releases shame's imprint on your body. Yoga does not have to be athletic or complicated.

The research indicating that yoga lessens trauma, depression and anxiety is mounting. Therapeutic yoga turns on your relaxation response and increases feelings of safety. In 2009, the *Harvard Mental Health Letter* reported that yoga can diminish the harmful effects of stress by modulating the stress response systems and decreasing physiological arousal. Bessel van der Kolk and colleagues (2014) conducted research that found that doing yoga reduced symptoms of PTSD in women who had not benefited from traditional mental health services. Yoga is increasingly recommended as complimentary treatment for military veterans with PTSD and for people experiencing depression. Streeter and associates (2017) found that yoga reduced symptoms of depression and reported that when the autonomic nervous system is balanced, the rest of the brain works better.

The simple practice that follows is designed to feel pleasant and be calming.

Practice ···

A Calming Yoga Practice

Dress comfortably and have a couple of beach towels or blankets nearby.

Begin in resting pose. Lie down on the floor with arms by your side, palms up. Let your feet splay slightly apart. Do what is needed for comfort: Place a folded towel under your neck or knees if desired. Rest here for several breaths or a few minutes.

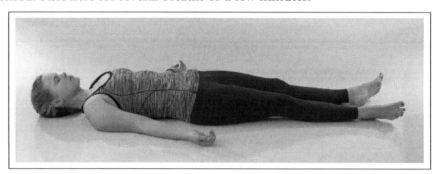

Banana pose: Stretch your arms over your head and to the right. Stretch your legs to the right, putting your body in the shape of a banana. If comfortable, hold your right wrist with your left hand. Keep both hips on the floor. Feel the stretch along the left side of your body. Take several breaths.

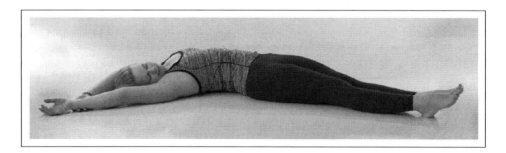

Switch sides. Stretch your arms overhead and to the left and your legs to the left. If comfortable, hold your left wrist with your right hand. Feel the stretch along the right side of your body. Take several breaths.

Knees to chest pose: Hug both knees to your chest. Rest quietly, or if you prefer, gently rock side to side. Take several breaths.

Hug your right knee to your chest, rest your left foot on the floor with your left knee in the air, or alternatively, extend your left leg along the floor. Take several breaths.

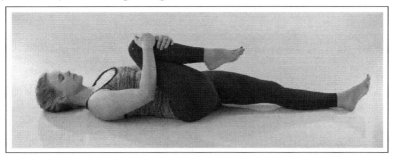

Hug your left knee to your chest, rest your right foot on the floor with your right knee in the air, or alternatively, extend your right leg along the floor. Take several breaths.

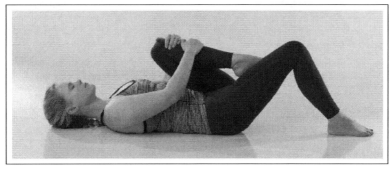

Pigeon pose right side: Rest your right ankle over left knee. Rest left foot on the floor or place hands behind left thigh and draw knee closer to chest. Take several breaths.

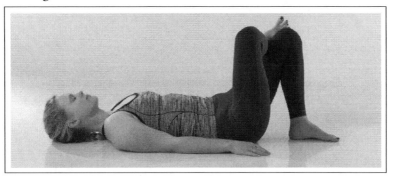

Pigeon pose left side: Rest your left ankle over right knee. Rest right foot on the floor or place hands behind right thigh and draw knee closer to chest. Take several breaths.

Cow and cat pose: Get on your hands and knees, with hands under shoulders and knees under hips. Inhale, gently lift your heart and head, and lift your tailbone up, arching your back. Exhale, bow your chin to your chest, and tuck your tailbone, rounding your back. Repeat a few times.

Sphinx pose: Lie on your tummy. Reach your toes gently toward the wall behind you. Place your elbows under your shoulders with your forearms parallel to each other. Enjoy this mild back bend. Take several breaths.

Select either child pose or puppy pose.

Child pose: Begin on hands and knees. Bend your knees, and rest your hips back toward your ankles and your head on the floor. If you prefer, place a folded blanket behind your knees. Either place your hands by your hips or rest them on the floor over your head. Rest for a minute or so.

Puppy pose: Begin on hands and knees. Stretch your arms out, and rest your hands on the floor in front of your body. Let your hips stay over your knees. Rest for a minute or so.

Legs up the wall: Place your hips close to a wall. Lift legs and rest the backs of your legs and heels against the wall. If comfortable, place a folded blanket under your hips for slight elevation. If preferred, place a folded blanket under your neck. Place your hands by your hips or extend them overhead and place them on the floor. Rest for a few minutes.

Knees to chest pose: Lie with your back on the floor. Bring both knees to chest, and wrap your arms around your legs. Gently rock side to side. Let your body become still. Rest for a minute or two.

Final resting pose: Extend your legs, stretching your body out on the floor. Let your feet be hip distance apart, and let your legs relax so that your feet splay out slightly. Let your hands rest on the floor by your hips, palms up. Breathe in, and as you breathe out, relax your toes and ankles. Breathe in, and as you breathe out, relax your fingers and wrists. Breathe in, and as you breathe out, relax your throat and your mouth. Remain in final resting pose for several minutes. Relax.

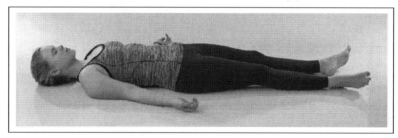

Wiggle your fingers and toes to become more alert. Inhale, and as you exhale, roll on your right side. Rest here for a few breaths. Inhale, and as you exhale, use your left hand to help lift your torso and come into a comfortable seated pose.

Practice even breathing. Breathe in for the count of five, and breathe out for the count of five. Repeat this breath practice five times.

Close your eyes. Envision the rising sun in the area between your eyebrows. Focus on the brilliant light. Sit for a couple of minutes, imagining sunlight in your forehead.

Close by chanting "Shanti, shanti, shantihi." This Sanskrit chant means "Peace, peace, peace."

Place your hands together over your heart and bow.

Increasing Interpersonal Safety—Yoga Group Classes

Believing that you are undesirable can contribute to the belief that others are not safe, at least to some degree. It is imperative to remember that unworthiness is a response to interpersonal belittling or neglect at home, in the community, and through racism, sexism, and other socially stigmatized identities. I restated the causes of unworthiness because it is easy to slip into believing that unworthiness is your fault.

It is daunting to risk vulnerability after you have been hurt. Your thinking mind and your nervous system have to learn to trust again. Fortunately your vagus nerve, the primary nerve of the parasympathetic nervous system, which relaxes your body, can be activated in some social settings. This is important, because optimal human living involves being able to trust and to tolerate intimacy.

You may want to participate in group yoga classes that combine yoga, meditation, and chanting. Scientifically speaking, doing so may hasten your healing. Stephen Porges (2011) writes that chanting with a group accesses the part of the vagus response associated with interpersonal safety. This means that your nervous system calms and feels safe while being in close physical proximity to others. Chanting is easy. Together, as a unit, the group breaths and sings simple phrases. You do not have to be a soloist, perform complex tasks, or talk about yourself to earn the right to belong.

There are many forms of yoga classes available. Look for gentle hatha yoga or trauma-informed classes. Both classes typically include breathing practices, meditation, brief chanting to end class, and yoga poses. You, as a participant, have your personal experience while moving and breathing in coordination with others. The breathing of the group synchronizes, threat systems relax, and the shared, yet individual, practice is enjoyable.

Practice ....

Explore Group Yoga Classes

When you are ready, explore yoga classes in your area. Try a few teachers and sample different groups to find one that is comfortable for you.

The Narrative of Unworthiness

There is an extraordinary 10-foot-tall, 5.5-ton solid gold Buddha statue in a temple in Thailand valued at more than 250 million dollars. Its story is remarkable. Made during the 13th to 14th century, it was plastered with stucco around the mid 1700s to protect it from an invading Burmese army. It survived the military attack, but the monks who covered it in plaster were killed, and the statue was lost to history for around 200 years. In 1955, during transport, the ropes broke and the statue fell to the ground, chipping and cracking the stucco. Imagine the monks shining flashlights into the cracks and discovering shining gold! The rest of the story is glorious. The stucco was removed and the Golden Buddha revealed. It remains on display at the Wat Traimit Temple in Bangkok.

This true accounting mirrors the process of recovering from the narrative of unworthiness. Healing is basically a chipping away at the stucco of low self-worth until the inner golden essence is revealed. The teachings of all wisdom traditions agree that human life is sacred, which means that your value is innate. Rather than earning inherent dignity and goodness, you uncover it.

Growing up involves solidifying a self-identity. It begins in earnest with the name you are given at birth. It continues on from there. You formulate attitudes about yourself, patterns in relationships, routines in your lifestyle, expectations about your future, and coping mechanisms for stress. You find a job or select a career and possibly become intimate partners with someone. By the time you are in your mid-twenties, identity becomes congealed. You have a predictable outlook on life, and you have a sense of who you are. Your identity becomes "just the way you are," "just who you are."

Unworthiness is a core story of not being good enough. You may feel okay about some aspects of who you are and not okay about others. Without knowing it, you may see yourself through a filter of inadequacy that mistakenly views your limitations and vulnerability as evidence of being flawed.

Unworthiness is also choiceless. In many respects, it is piled on, just as the stucco was applied to cover the Buddha statue. "Not good enough, not deserving" is not who you are.

Here is the bottom line: Any identity that does not recognize that all people share inherent human worth is false and painful. Look at the types of suffering with which unworthiness is associated: a damaging inner critic, depression, anxiety, secrecy, a sense of powerlessness, perfectionism, and high need for control.

Healing requires that you recognize the story of false identity as an untruth. See it for what it is—an old, historical identity. Then you can begin to relate to the narrative of unworthiness with kindness, curiosity, and much less self-blame.

This next practice chisels away at the narrative of unworthiness and builds on the practice of writing the story of "who I am" that you did in Chapter 4. Words are powerful, so be gentle with this practice and remember Pema Chodron's teaching about you as the sky and everything as the weather. Your story is the weather. You experience the weather, yet who you are cannot be defined by it.

Practice ....

Recognize Your "Story Of Me" as Not True

Write a summary phrase of the "story of me." Envision your true identity as golden and your story as mere covering. Above all, keep in mind that your old story is not who you are in essence—you cannot be reduced to such words. After completing your summary phrase, write a statement such as, "Old story, simply not true" to acknowledge that your story of "not enough" is false, inaccurate, and incomplete.

_____

_____

_____

_____

Your New Narrative

Now the intrigue begins. If you are not your story, then who are you? At birth, you were an intelligent, responsive being of awareness who was filled with human potential. Then, along came rapid learning and language and experiences that informed your personality. Finally, here you are. The question remains: Who are you?

The yogic self-inquiry method of the Hindu sage Ramana Maharshi (2000) points to your essence, the sacred you illustrated by the Golden Buddha story. He taught a simple practice of inquiry that consists of simply asking, "Who am I?" to yourself. Then, you respond. Answer by stating the roles you play in your family; your body's age, shape, and health; social status; educational level; personality type; work experiences; hobbies; talents; beliefs about your worthiness; and on and on. As you know, experiences come and go, physical bodies change, roles relating to family life are temporary, jobs transition, and hobbies evolve. In truth, you cannot accurately be defined by things that are so fleeting.

Answering the question becomes a journey into the unknown. Confronted by mystery as you continue to inquire, you may turn to philosophical and spiritual answers. Ramana Maharshi's answer to the question is that you are awareness or consciousness—who you are is beyond words. The quote by the French philosopher and Jesuit priest Pierre Teilhard de

Chardin, "You are not a human being in search of a spiritual experience. You are a spiritual being immersed in a human experience," expresses a similar idea.

Having a narrative is natural. After all, we humans are story makers. Plus, it is in our nature to define ourselves. So, come up with a new narrative that honors human dignity—something as simple as "I am a sacred being."

Following is an opportunity to develop a story of who you are that affirms human goodness.

Practice ....

Developing a "Story of Me" That Recognizes Innate Human Value

Answer the question "Who am I?" at least 20 times or enough times to exhaust obvious responses.

_____

_____

_____

_____

_____

_____

_____

_____

Write a few loving narratives to answer the question "Who am I?" Select the most appealing to use as your new narrative.

_____

_____

_____

_____

What Matters Most to You

Unworthiness and shame stifle your ability to explore what matters most, because the third emotional motivational system (the drive, vitality system discussed in Chapter 1) is usurped by the threat system. It channels the energy of vitality into safety, nonexposure, control, invisibility, perfectionism, avoidance, and/or other maneuvers that ward off the possibility of embarrassment. As a result, your deeper desires may be pushed aside.

You can access and follow inner guidance. You can learn to treat your emotions with mercy, comfort your body, relax your nervous system, and relate to thoughts such as "Something is wrong with me" wisely. When your mind is quieter, you can hear your deeper yearnings. When your body is calmer, you can redirect the energy that had been expended on anxiety toward what truly matters to you. Additionally, you can use self-compassion to help yourself take small steps.

What is important begins to shift as you heal. According to Folletto, Hopper, and colleagues (2015), you begin to "seek true goods" or pursue deeper values. Matters of the heart, including family, beauty, service, creativity, health, human rights, and peace, become more central.

The time comes to inquire into your innermost desires. A direct and poignant way to do so is by writing your own eulogy. When you write your eulogy, you come into intimate contact with mortality, potentiality, and the precious nature of life, even with its difficulties and challenges.

As a culture, we are uncomfortable with death. Therefore, the thought of writing a eulogy may seem daunting initially. Yet the idea of writing a eulogy is more unsettling than actually writing one is.

For now, read through the practice directions. You may choose to just read and spend a few minutes in contemplation as you first approach this practice. Write a eulogy when you feel ready.

To prepare, contemplate the end of your life in some unknown future. From that vantage point, make the following affirmations, even if you don't yet believe them.

- Your life mattered.
- You followed your heart.
- You made the world a better place.

From this imagined future place, write your eulogy. Allow this to be an ideal eulogy, one that factors in the affirmations just listed while honoring where you are now. Be generous and true to yourself.

Practice ....

Writing Your Ideal Eulogy
To Discover Your Deepest Desires

This is a four-step practice.

1.   Write the following statement.

This is a eulogy for [your name]. His/her life mattered.

_____

_____

_____

2.   Write a eulogy.

_____

_____

_____

_____

_____

_____

_____

_____

_____

_____

_____

_____

3. Read your eulogy. Circle words that reveal your deeper desires.

4. Complete the following statement.

What mattered most to [fill in your name] was:

_____

_____

_____

_____

"What mattered most" is a statement of your deeper desires. Revisit and refine your eulogy periodically to keep the winds of grace pushing you in the direction of your potential.

CHAPTER 8

Increasing Contentment and Inner Peace

Benefits & Clinician Notes

✓ Learning to be friendly with self

✓ Accepting life as it is

✓ Finding contentment in the midst of life

✓ Living in present moment

This chapter educates your patients about how to take things in stride, make friends with their lives, and practice gratitude. It teaches them to lean on what Mukunda Stiles (2002) calls four heart capacities in the yoga tradition. They are compassion, friendliness, equanimity, and happiness/joy. Although learning to cultivate these comes later in the healing process, doing so is critical for wellbeing, because focusing your mind on these strengths establishes inner serenity.

First, some perspective. Thich Nhat Hahn (2014) teaches that suffering and joy are utterly connected, like the palm and back of your hand. Without suffering, there is no joy and without joy, there is no suffering.

To make this concept concrete, imagine that a beloved grandparent gave you a beautifully crafted ceramic bowl many years ago. Most likely, you would feel joy just holding it. Now picture the bowl on the floor, broken into several pieces. Most likely, you would feel sad looking at it. Without joy, you would not feel sad when your treasured bowl is dropped. This simple analogy links joy and sorrow and sets the stage for the transformation that arises when original beauty and brokenness are both honored and loved.

The bowl picture illustrates a Japanese art form called Kintsugi, which means "golden joinery." It is a process that reconnects pottery pieces with gold-infused glue. When the glue dries, the gold shines through the seams that hold the broken pieces together. The brokenness is illuminated, not hidden, and after being repaired, the bowl is considered to be even more beautiful.

To glue the pottery, you have to utilize the heart capacities named previously. Remember that the first capacity, compassion, includes the desire to alleviate suffering (taught in Chapter 6). Obviously, you have to want to fix the bowl.

Kintsugi becomes possible when you face the reality that the bowl is broken. This is accepting what is, an aspect of friendliness. Next, you need to be composed when lining the broken pieces with glue so that you don't make a big mess. This is being calm in the midst of the storm, a feature of equanimity. Finally, because you treasure the bowl, you are happy to be able to restore it, place it back on the shelf, and enjoy it again. This is happiness with having what is desired, which is essential for joy.

There is some parallel between repairing pottery and healing human wounds. Yet, personal transformation is not a one-time glue job. As a human, you are complex and healing is an ongoing process of intentionally creating and utilizing healthy neuropathways in your brain. The pathways of the heart, the focus of this chapter, become well worn and preferred as a result of repeated practice. As Swami Satchidananda taught (1978), what you think about becomes your reality.

This clinical example illustrates the advantages of developing these capacities. In Chapter 1, I introduced you to Susan, the lovely woman who felt hope after learning that her suicidal ideation was a trauma memory. One day, she announced that since she was going to live, she might as well focus on being happy. In the following sessions, we explored releasing what she couldn't control, such as other people's behaviors. She also let go of family members and friends who perpetuated old trauma, which was of great help to her. Susan focused more on living in the present and enjoying life. For her, happiness is a lifestyle of gardening, traveling with her husband, being with people of depth, positively affecting the lives of children, visiting family, and doing some pleasant activity each day. Toward the end of our work together, she said she mostly appreciates her life, feels stronger, and no longer has thoughts of wishing to not be alive.

This chapter empowers your patients to join Susan in being a Kintsugi master of life. It helps them live day by day by day. It also teaches them the skills that foster inner peace.

Friendliness—Acceptance of What Is

Wrestling with yourself is no way to Kintsugi, or lovingly glue yourself back together again. It is easy to be friendly with what you adore and approve of yet not so easy to be friendly with what you fear and disapprove of, especially within yourself. Yet, unfriendliness within perpetuates self-loathing and emotional pain. Fundamentally, it keeps you in conflict with yourself.

Internal fighting is no way to cultivate happiness. Martin Luther King, Jr. said, "Darkness cannot drive out darkness; only light can do that. Hate cannot drive out hate; only love can do that." Exiling or hiding parts of your personality in a dungeon doesn't increase inner ease.

Friendliness weaves together a gentle "hello" to what is arising, followed by a "yes" to what supports you, when you need support. Here is what friendliness sounds like: When things go wrong, softly say something like, "Hello difficulty, I know you are here." Then, support yourself the way a friend would. Whisper phrases like, "Yes, things like this happen," "This is hard, not what I want," or "Yes, this is part of living."

The invitation is to do this without too much frustration or thoughts like "life is so hard." But if the old habit of grumbling arises again, softly say something like, "Hello, grumbling, I know you are here." Breathe and whisper, "Yes, life has ups and downs," or other words that comfort.

Friendliness with what is is a practice of nonresistance, not of passivity. It preserves life energy because you do not waste energy denying, pretending, ignoring, and/or arguing with what is. And when you do protest, simply take that into the friendliness practice. Say, "Hello protesting, I know you are here." Breathe, then offer supportive words such as, "Yes, this will pass," and "Thank goodness for the people I love."

Practice ···

Friendliness

Friendliness is whispering "hello" to what is arising and then "yes" to that which gives support when needed. In this three-part practice, first say "hello" to what you are attracted to. Second, say "hello" to what you find challenging. Third, say "yes" to expressions of support.

In the space below, list things, such a good weather and delicious food, to which you can easily say "hello."

_____

_____

_____

_____

In the space below, list things, such as illness and arguments, you find it challenging to say "hello" to.

_____

_____

_____

_____

In the space below, list supportive phrases, such as, "One day at a time," to which you can say "yes," even in the midst of difficulty. If "yes" doesn't feel possible, come back to this section after completing this chapter.

_____

_____

_____

_____

Equanimity

Equanimity refers to your ability to be level-headed and composed, especially in difficult situations. Simply stated, it means being calm in the midst of the storm. You have equanimity when you don't fall apart when things get tough.

Equanimity is made up of regulating and taking care of your emotions (Chapters 3 and 5), coupled with your attitude toward life. For example, when navigating through a difficult transition, breathe through fear and say, "This is just the way it is." Doing so helps you to stay on course, step by step, and preserves your energy.

Following are four skillful perspectives that support your ability to cope with life as it is, during good times and bad times. They are:

- Accepting what you cannot change and changing what you can
- Living in the present
- Impermanence in life
- Reverence for life

These views are interconnected and sustained by each other. Perhaps more importantly, they are valuable perspectives that make life easier and more enjoyable. They are presented in individual sections for your inquiry so that you can give each of them due consideration.

Accepting What You Cannot Change and Changing What You Can

The Serenity Prayer by theologian Reinhold Niebuhr (Sifton, 2003), "God grant me the serenity to accept what I cannot change, courage to change what I can, and wisdom to know the difference," is a pointed reminder about the power of focusing your efforts on what you can change, and you can only change yourself. It takes perseverance, however. Step by step, you can change how you take care of your emotions, relate to your thoughts, communicate, and what you chose to focus on.

Plus, keep in mind the reality of the social brain. Changes that you make in your lifestyle may well benefit others. The possibility that your positive changes impact others is reflected in these famous words by Mahatma Ghandi: "If we could change ourselves, the tendencies in the world would also change."

Practice ··

Accepting What You Cannot Change and Making Desired Changes

List things, events, and aspects of other people that you may wish to change but recognize you cannot.

_____

_____

_____

_____

List outdated behavioral habits, old thoughts, and coping skills that you would like to let go of. This is a joyful practice when you realize that you are listing habits that are not who you truly are, so do not scold yourself.

_____

_____

_____

_____

On the next page, list a couple of desired changes you would like to make. Then, list small behavioral steps you can take daily that support your desired change. Here are examples.

- Lowering anxiety. A small behavioral step would be practicing gentle yoga for 10 to 15 minutes daily.

- Abstaining from drinking alcohol. A small behavioral step would be attending an Alcoholics Anonymous meeting.

- Decreasing irritation. A small behavioral step would be taking a daily walk.

- Quieting your mind. A small behavioral step would be sitting in meditation for 10 to 15 minutes in the morning.

- Preparing varied meal menus. A small behavioral step would be to read one new recipe daily.

- Reading for pleasure. A small behavioral step would be sitting in your favorite chair and reading for 15 minutes daily.

_____

_____

_____

_____

P.S. When you forget or slip, and you will, forgive yourself and start over again.

Living in the Present

Thinking about yesterday and tomorrow takes you away from today. Worry and rumination place you in another timeframe or era and take you away from the present. Since your mind's default network naturally drifts off, the practice of returning to the present, where life is fresh and real, is very beneficial.

How you live today influences your future. You literally change your tomorrows by changes you make in the present. For instance, eat a piece of fruit mindfully daily, and over time, you will eat healthier foods regularly because you have established new neuropathways.

You can choose to focus on your actions, senses, or physical sensations to come back to present moment awareness. Mindful eating, perhaps of an apple, is a great example of a pleasing present moment. Paying attention as you retrieve an apple from the refrigerator and rinse it off is awareness of actions. Focusing on tasting the apple is awareness of sensory input, and focusing on chewing and swallowing is awareness of bodily sensation.

Eat something that tastes delicious in this way, and your present moment experience is rich and complete. Nothing more is needed for your enjoyment.

Practice ....

Enjoying the Present Moment While Making Desired Changes

Review your desired changes from the previous section. If your small behavioral step is walking, practice doing so in a way that allows you to enjoy the present moment. Pay attention to the sensations of the heel-to-toe movement as you step along. Thich Nhat Hahn taught a mantra, "Breathing in I have arrived, breathing out I am home," to recite during mindful walking. It is also a reminder that wherever you go, you are at home in the present moment.

In the space below, journal about how you can add present moment awareness focus to the small behavioral changes that you listed in the previous practice.

_____

_____

_____

Impermanence

Appreciate impermanence, and you establish a firm bedrock for equanimity. Our human lifespan is limited, which our culture is reluctant to discuss, unfortunately. Keep mortality close in mind, and you reap the following three tremendous rewards.

- Knowing how precious each fleeting moment is. This helps you to value yourself, your relationships, and the time you have on earth.
- Knowing that tough times are transitory. The saying "This too shall pass," is a poignant reminder that circumstances are temporary.
- Knowing that nothing remains the same. This helps you treasure and not cling, since things take form, fall apart, and come together again in new ways.

Thich Nhat Hahn is often quoted as having said, "Thanks to impermanence, everything is possible." The possibility for healing is based on the truth that you and your brain can change. It is time to become more friendly with impermanence.

Practice ....

Exploring Benefits of Impermanence

List how the perspective that life is precious because it is not forever is helpful for you.

_____

_____

_____

_____

List how the perspective that tough times are temporary is helpful for you.

_____

_____

_____

_____

List how the perspective that things keep changing is helpful for you.

_____

_____

_____

_____

Reverence for Life

Most likely, you have had moments of sensing something greater than the mundane. After all, the precious nature of life is not hidden. It is obvious in newborn babies, the stillness of the wilderness, and the poetry of mystics.

Undeniably, there is sanctity in life. Following is a brief list of ways it shows up.

- It shines when people triumph over adversity and come together during times of tragedy.
- It speaks through voices that advocate for human rights and sing uplifting songs.
- It works through lifesaving medical research and astonishing architecture.

Trauma can erode your capacity to sense the miraculous. This is because a nervous system tightly wired for threat may be less attuned to this greater goodness. Healing involves discovering and deeply respecting its presence. Then, you have reverence for life. Then, you connect your humanity with the sacred. Then, you no longer just tend to suffering—you also tune into awe.

Practice ....

Reconnecting To the Presence of Greater Goodness

Write about times when you sensed the presence of greater goodness. Consider peak experiences in nature or with loved ones, inspired words that changed you, and times of stillness that felt holy.

_____

_____

_____

_____

Explore ways you could intentionally appreciate goodness. Consider praying, meditating, chanting, singing, walking in nature, reading sacred books, doing yoga, saying grace before meals, gardening, painting, playing a musical instrument, writing gratitude lists.

_____

_____

_____

Surrender

When you surrender to a higher power or to greater goodness, you release your misguided need to go it alone. You admit that you need help. Said differently, thinking that you don't need support is simply inaccurate. It also generates stress. Saying, "Let go, let God," or making another statement that feels true to you allows you to lean on wisdom and strength greater than your own, and that creates calm.

Surrender is not about irresponsibility, resignation, or passivity. Nor is it the nervous system response of tonic immobility. In fact, it is the opposite of numbing body and mind: It wakes you up to the presence of goodness. Surrender is a devotional act of faith in God, mystery, spirit, or love and, as such, does not require religious affiliation.

You may first experience surrender when your ability to cope by yourself is exhausted. You have probably had times when, in desperation, all you could do was fall on your knees and call out to that in which you might not yet have faith. Those moments of yielding and pleading, "Thy will, not my will," or "You handle this, I cannot," may draw you into spirituality.

Surrender makes you aware of higher consciousness in times both good and bad. When times are rough, you cry out. When times are wonderful, you give thanks. Surrender is releasing ownership of sorrow, pride, and joy and fundamentally is an acknowledgment that you are never on your own.

Practice ···

Reconnecting to Surrendering to Pervasive Goodness

Journal times of surrender when you fell on your knees and how those experiences impacted you. Be gentle. Focus more on recalling connection and less on any painful circumstances at the time.

_____

_____

_____

Describe your way, if you have one, of surrendering to higher power or pervasive goodness, including the words that you use.

_____

_____

_____

_____

Choosing to be Content with What Is

Seek contentment in the midst of your daily life if you want to be happier. Pause periodically throughout the day and look for something to which you are happy to say "yes." Cultivating contentment doesn't mean that you like everything that is occurring. It means that you face what is occurring and also choose to focus on what is pleasing and/or beneficial in ordinary life. It also teaches that while more and upgraded material possessions may be useful, they are not the key to happiness.

Looking for what makes you feel contented counters the brain's tendency to gravitate toward the negative. Focus more on what is going well than what is going wrong, and you decrease dissatisfaction. Plus, you create healthier neuropathways.

In nearly every moment, you can focus on something that increases your contentment.

- Comfortable breath, fingers and toes that work, not having a headache
- A loved one's voice, a cat purring, a dog snoring, a baby sleeping
- The smell of coffee, food in the refrigerator, laundry folded, a reliable car
- The sun shining in, raindrops falling, a breeze blowing

Practice ....

Increasing Contentment With Life as it is

In this moment, name what you can focus on to increase your contentment with life as it is.

_____

_____

_____

_____

Gratitude

If you want to be happier, practice gratitude, because grateful people are genuinely happier. According to David Steindl-Rast (2016), it is not happy people who are naturally grateful, it is the other way around. He adds that you cannot be grateful for everything, such as violence, oppression, and tragedy. Yet, even during difficulties, there is something to be grateful for, whether it is the opportunity to practice patience or stand up for convictions or learn to receive support. So, in every moment, you can be grateful for something.

He explains that true gratitude is associated with something valuable that is freely given and that the most sacred gift is each moment. Each moment is here to enjoy and/or is an opportunity for contributing, maturing, or loving. And when you miss a moment, there is no need to punish yourself, because there is the next moment.

He offers a method for harnessing gratitude. The method is called "Stop, Look, Go."

- "Stop" is the instruction to pause, slow down, get quiet, and take a breath. You can't take in the moment when you rush, are distracted, or are lost in thought.
- "Look" is the instruction to sense into your heart so you can receive the gift.
- "Go" is the instruction to move toward gratitude, which often is simply to enjoy the moment!

Practice ....

A Reminder To Be Grateful

Practicing gratitude is a glorious exercise, so do what you can do to increase the likelihood that you will repeatedly practice. Props and prompts help you form new habits. Be creative and come up with a catchy reminder, something as simple as a red, yellow, and green gratitude stoplight signifying "stop" "look" "go", that encourages you to practice. Alternatively, consider making a colorful sign or plaque, a framed card, or a calligraphy note or preset a daily cell phone notification.

Take some time and enjoy this as an art project. Make your personalized reminder and display it where you will see it frequently. Support yourself in practicing gratitude, remembering that it takes reinforcement to make changes. Do this for your happiness.

Ongoing Healing Journey

There is no final destination at which to arrive nor anything that marks the end of healing. For the rest of your life, you can practice being aware, being your own best friend, and being guided by your heart's truest desires. You can refer back to the skill sets in this workbook to support you along the way.

In closing, I highlight my inner journey while writing to illustrate the ongoing nature of transformation. In the early summer of 2017, halfway through writing the manuscript, my combined home and work schedule was intense. Overwhelm began waking me up in the middle of the night, like it last did in 2009 after my husband was severely injured in an accident. Coincidentally, this occurred while writing the chapter on taking care of emotions. I practiced giving MERCY to overwhelm in the wee hours, resting in bed until it receded. Although overwhelm has not visited me since, it may again, because sometimes life is difficult and I am a vulnerable human being. However, I know that if it does, I have a well-tested resource waiting in reserve, and for that I am grateful.

Then, I wrote the section on relating to the inner critic, an aspect of personality that I have inquired into for a long time. It is fairly dormant in me, thanks to years of yoga, meditation, and study. So, I was surprised when I was awakened in the night by the words, "Oh, my goodness, my inner critic is Grandma Mae!" Tucked comfortably in bed, I chuckled and reminisced about my long-deceased paternal grandmother. Hers was a tough life. She walked from Michigan to Iowa, had 13 children, lived in poverty, and was scorned by her rural neighbors. No wonder she admonished me for sewing cute clothes, being a small-town school cheerleader, and trying to fit in with my classmates. She did not seem happy and apparently could not envision her granddaughter having a different kind of life than the one she lived.

Poverty, my father's mental illness, my mother's disorganization, and my family's low social status helped form my inner critic. But, I now have a new name for and deeper understanding of it and a new sorrow for the plight of my grandmother. As a result, I experience more internal ease and acceptance of my historical patterns.

In early fall, I wrote the section on the eulogy. I have written more than a dozen of them over the past 20 years, and each has been illuminating. The eulogy I wrote during retreat in November 2017 highlighted that what matters most to me is remembering the sanctity in everyone with whom I interact: myself, family, friends, strangers, and now you. Sometimes, I forget and fall back into believing that I am my historical story and that others are their historical stories. But, thanks to a framed photo in my bathroom and a card on my desk that remind me we are sacred beings, I soon remember again what my heart knows to be true, which is that we are inherently worthy.

I am grateful for intentionally cultivated neuropathways in my mind, and I trust the power of mindfulness practices. My hope for you is that you align yourself with the strength of your brain and the capacities of your heart and, most of all, that you remain faithful to your healing journey.

In the yoga tradition, group classes end in the following way. We slightly bow, place our hands in prayer pose, and say "namaste," a Hindu salutation that is translated as, "I bow to the divine in you." I close this workbook by placing my hands at my heart and whispering "namaste" to you.

References

Buckner, R. l., Andres-Hanna, J. R., & Schacter, D. L. (2008). The brain's default network: Anatomy, function, and relevance to disease. *Annals of the New York Academy of Science, 1124,* 1–38.

Chodron, P. (2001). *The Wisdom of no Escape and the Path of Loving-Kindness.* Boulder: Shambhala.

Chodron, P. (2013). *Living Beautifully with Uncertainty and Change.* Boulder: Shambhala.

Davidson, R., & Begley, S. (2012). *The Emotional Life of Your Brain: How Its Unique Patterns Affect the Way You Think, Feel, and Live and How You Can Change Them.* London: Penguin Books.

Desbordes, G., Negli, L. T., Pace, T. W., Wallace, B. A., Raison, C. L., & Schwartz, E. L. (2012). Effects of mindful attention and compassion meditation training on amygdala response to emotional stimuli in an ordinary, non-meditative state. *Frontiers in Human Neuroscience, 6,* 292.

Dispenza, J. (2007). *Evolve Your Brain: The Science of Changing Your Mind.* Deerfield Beach, FL: Health Communications, Inc.

Feldman, L. (2017). *How Emotions are Made: The Secret Life of the Brain.* New York: Houghton Mifflin Harcourt.

Felitti, V. J., Anda, R. F., Nordenberg, D., Williamson, D. F., Spitz, A. M., Edwards, V., … Marks, J. S., et al. (1998). Relationship of childhood abuse and household dysfunction to many of the leading causes of death in adults. *American Journal of Preventive Medicine, 14*(2), 245–258.

Finlay, B., and Uchiyama, R. (2015). Developmental mechanisms channeling cortical evolution. *Trends in Neurosciences, 38*(2), 69–76.

Folletto V., Briere, J., Rozelle, D., and Hopper, J. (Eds). (2015). *Mindfulness-Oriented Intervention for Trauma: Integrating Contemplative Practices.* New York: The Guilford Press.

Frewen, P., and Lanius, R. (2015). *Healing the Traumatized Self: Consciousness, Neuroscience, Treatment.* New York: Norton & Company.

Germer, C. (2009). *The Mindful Path to Self-Compassion: Freeing Yourself from Destructive Thoughts and Emotions.* New York: The Guilford Press.

Gilbert, P., and Chodon, K. (2014). *Mindful Compassion.* Oakland: New Harbinger Publications.

Goyal, M., Singh, S., Sibinga, E. M. S., Gould, N. F., Rowland-Seymour, A., Sharma, R., … et al. (2014). Meditation programs for psychological stress and well-being: A systematic review and meta-analysis, *JAMA Internal Medicine, 174*(3), 357–368.

Hamlin, J.K., Wynn, K., and Bloom, P. (2007). Social evaluation by preverbal infants. *Nature,* (7169): 557-9.

Hanson, R. (2009). *Buddha's Brain: The Practical Neuroscience of Happiness, Love, and Wisdom.* Oakland: New Harbinger Publications, Inc.

Herman, J. (1992). *Trauma and Recovery: The Aftermath of Violence—from Domestic Abuse to Political Terror.* New York: Basic Books.

Kilingsworth, M., and Gilbert, D. (2010). A wandering mind is an unhappy mind. *Science, 330,* 932.

Kirste, I., Nicola, Z., Kronenberg, G., Walker, T. L., Liu, R. C., and Kempermann, G. (2015). Is silence golden? Effects of auditory stimuli and their absence on adult hippocampal neurogenesis. *Brain Structure Function, 220*(2), 1221–1228.

Levine, S. (2015). *Trauma and Memory: Brain and Body in a Search for the Living Past.* Berkeley: North Atlantic Books.

Maharshi, R. (2000). *Talks with Ramana Maharshi.* Carlsbad, CA: Inner Directions Foundation.

Merzenich, M. (2013). *Soft-Wired: How the New Science of Brain Plasticity Can Change Your Life*. San Francisco: Parnassus Publishing, LLC.

Moullin, S., Waldfogel, J., and Washbrook, E. (2014). *Baby Bonds: Parenting, Attachment and a Secure Base for Children*. London: Sutton Trust.

Neff, K. (2015). *Self-Compassion: The Proven Power of Being Kind to Yourself*. New York: HarperCollins Publishers.

NurrieStearns, M. (1999). Pride, strength, and humility: An interview with Thomas Keating. *Personal Transformation Magazine, 8*(1), 39–45.

Ogden, P., and Fisher, J. (2015). *Sensorimotor Psychotherapy*. New York: W. W. Norton and Company.

Porges, S. (2011). *Polyvagal Theory: Neurophysiological Foundations of Emotions, Attachment, Communication, and Self-Regulation*. New York: W. W. Norton & Company, Inc.

Siegel, D. (2010). *Mindsight: The New Science of Personal Transformation*. New York: Bantam Books.

Sifton, E. (2003). *The Serenity Prayer: Faith and Politics in Times of Peace and War*. New York: W. W. Norton & Company.

Steindl-Rast, D. (2016). *Stop-Look-Go: A Grateful Practice Workbook and Gratitude Journal*. New York: Wink Books, Inc.

Stiles, M. (2002). *Yoga Sutras of Patanjali: With Great Respect and Love*. Boston: Red Wheel/Weiser, LLC.

Streeter, C. C., Gerbarg, P. L., Whitfield, T. H., Owen, L., Johnston, J., Silveri, M. M, … Jensen, J. E. (2017). Treatment of major depressive disorder with Iyengar yoga and coherent breathing: A randomized controlled dosing study. *Journal of Alternative and Complementary Medicine, 23*(3), 201–207.

Swami Satchidananda. (1978). *The Yoga Sutras of Patanjali*. Buckingham, VA: Integral Yoga Publications.

Thich Nhat Hahn. (2014). *No Mud, No Lotus: The Art of Transforming Suffering*. Berkeley: Parallax Press.

Turunen, T. (2014). *Trauma recovery after a school shooting: The role of theory-based psychosocial care and attachment in facilitating recovery* (Doctoral dissertation). Tampere University Press, Tampere, Finland.

van der Kolk, B. (2015). *The Body Keeps the Score*. New York: Penguin House.

van der Kolk, B., Stone, L., West, J., Rhodes, A., Emerson, D., Suvak, M., and Spinazzola, J. (2014). Yoga as an adjunctive treatment for posttraumatic stress disorder: A randomized controlled trial. *Journal of Clinical Psychiatry, 75*(6), 559–565.

Warneken, F., and Tomasello, M. (2009). The roots of human altruism. *British Journal of Psychology, 100*(3), 455–471.

Warren, R., Smeets, E., and Neff, K. (2016). Risk and resilience: Being compassionate to oneself is associated with emotional resilience and psychological well-being. *Current Psychiatry, 15*(12), 19–32.

Made in the USA
San Bernardino, CA
06 January 2020